Journeying with the Bible

Don Rooney

LITURGICAL PRESS
Collegeville, Minnesota

www.litpress.org

1   2   3   4   5   6   7   8

Library of Congress Cataloging-in-Publication Data

Rooney, Don, 1953–
    Journeying with the Bible / Don Rooney.
       p.   cm.
    ISBN 0-8146-2896-6 (alk. paper)
    1. Bible—Hermeneutics.   I. Title.

  BS476.R66   2005
  200.6'.01—dc21   2002075502

To
Walter and Mary Vasitas

Contents

Introduction

We are familiar with their names: The Ritz Carlton, Holiday Inn, Best Western, Motel 6. Even though hotels come in different designs and sizes, they each offer their services to a specific clientele. Some are for families, others cater to the business traveler. Some have a pool or include a restaurant. One will offer room service while another will even do your laundry overnight. While they each offer their own brand of hospitality, they do have some similarities. There is a bed, a sink, closet space, and, most often, a Bible. The one book translated into more languages and with more copies in print than any other book in the world. Most every hotel has one.

Whether you come to church each week, you are someone who has been away and is returning, or even if you're just starting out in the faith, the ideas in this book are for you. As you discover all that the Bible has to say, you will be more and more drawn to its words and the God who speaks them. You won't have to travel to a hotel to take a journey. Your journey will begin without even leaving the house.

Remember the last time you heard music on the radio or on a CD? All of us can listen and enjoy the sound of the instruments. However, the person who has taken music lessons on a particular instrument will often appreciate what is heard in a way that another listener might not. While it is true that a person does not have to be well versed in music to enjoy what is heard, knowledge can help appreciate it more fully. As you learn, you tend to notice things that the casual observer does not.

The same could be said of the Bible. But here, there is more at stake than in listening to music. If a listener mistakes one instrument for another, not much damage is done. But as soon as we recall that the Bible is God's Word, God speaking to us, then the stakes are higher. We want to be more careful that we "get it right." This is not only for our own benefit, but is helpful for others as well. Have you ever acted in a certain way because of what you believed God meant to teach us in a particular passage of the Bible? If so, then you know the Bible does influence what we believe and how we deal with those around us, and appreciating what it says can make a difference.

> Therefore, since everything asserted by the inspired authors or sacred writers must be held to be asserted by the Holy Spirit, it follows that the books of Scripture must be acknowledged as teaching firmly, faithfully and without error that truth which God wanted put into the sacred writings for the sake of our salvation.
>
> —Vatican Council II, *Dei Verbum* 11

> . . . and that from infancy you have known [the] sacred scriptures, which are capable of giving you wisdom for salvation through faith in Christ Jesus.
>
> —2 Timothy 3:15

Not only as individuals do we depend on Scripture, but also as communities. So much of what is believed, taught, and practiced in the Catholic faith finds its mirror in this collection of sacred books. How we interpret what is in the Bible is significant to the Jewish and Christian religions and those who participate in them. This is exactly as it should be.

Why read a book about the Bible? In fact, some might suggest that reading a book about interpreting Scripture is unnecessary or not especially helpful. After all, can't we just read the Bible itself and come to understand it on our own? Isn't all this just common sense? Let's look at some examples:

> While reading a report of an accident an insurance adjuster comes across this statement: "I had been driving my car for forty years when I fell asleep at the wheel and had an accident." Had the driver really been at the wheel nonstop for forty years before getting drowsy? Of course not. Common sense tells the adjuster exactly what the writer means.

> You're in the drive-thru lane at a McDonald's restaurant placing your order. It's a busy day and there are four cars between you and the pick-up window. No one is moving. After you order you are told, "That will be $5, please pull up." Common sense tells you that you don't drive around the cars in front of you to get your order. You have to wait for them to move first.

As with any other subject, common sense has its place in daily life as well as when we read the Bible. But there are things helpful to learn about Scripture that will not just come to us automatically. Sometimes we need a guide.

This book is written in everyday English to help you come to a better understanding of God's Word and what God says to us. To be sure, it is only one of many books that have been written, and so I am not trying to cover every aspect of the Bible here. However, it is my hope that the focus and approach that are offered here will provide you with some thoughtful reflections and help you in your own appreciation of the Scriptures.

The approach I have taken here is a very practical one. It can be applied anytime you read the Bible to help understand what it is that God is communicating. For most people, that is the purpose for which they read and pray the Scriptures.

This book is based on three basic beliefs:

1. The Bible is in a real sense the Word of God. Part of what makes understanding the Bible important is because once we come to conclusions about what God has said, if it is indeed God's Word, then we are compelled to believe and act. In this respect the Bible is unique when compared with other books about religion or theology.

2. God's guidance has been expressed in and through human words. Human authors made use of their own talents, abilities, and resources, in cooperation with God, in composing these sacred books. Because of this, the Bible shares some of the same characteristics of other literature.

3. Christians of all faiths and of every generation are called upon to make God's Word come alive in their own lives. God speaks to each one of us through the Word. The Bible is for you.

While these notions are certainly consistent within the tradition of the Catholic Church, other denominations may find them acceptable as well. If these three ideas correspond to what you hold true, then I think you will find the approach used here a helpful one.

We are all called to make a journey with God. There is a real sense in which the Bible is a type of guidebook that helps us on our way. This book you are reading now will offer five chapters composed of steps that can be used to make this journey:

Prepare: Before you start to read the Bible, you have to select which edition or translation you will use. Chapter 1 briefly sets out some introductory ideas to help you become more familiar with the different texts of the Bible that are available. A description of how the Bible is organized is included.

Consider: Chapter 2 looks at the question of whether or not the Bible should be interpreted. It is important to consider this idea, since it forms the basis for what we will do when we read the Scriptures. As you read this chapter you'll find an interactive approach you can work with to help when you interpret God's Word.

Interpret: Chapter 3 acts on the premise that the Bible is to be interpreted. But if this is so, how do we know if we're doing this in a way that is compatible with our faith and tradition? This section includes twelve guidelines that can be used to help anyone praying over the Scriptures to feel more confident about interpreting God's Word authentically.

Discover: Just as we can move in our relationships from being an acquaintance to being a friend, this same development can happen with the Bible. We can move from being able to recognize a passage as belonging to the Bible, to seeing beneath the surface something valuable that others may not notice. Chapter 4 describes some techniques you can use to explore beyond the most obvious meaning of a passage.

Reflect: Chapter 5 will provide some examples of how the ideas in this book can be used in such a way that the Bible will become a great place to go for help, insight, and prayer. Passages of Scripture are presented along with an interpretation and a question for reflection. At some point the Bible must come to life and influence what we do. This section will provide a way of using the Bible that you can imitate to breathe new life into the Scriptures.

Chapter 1

Prepare

The Books of the Bible

The names of the Old Testament books are as follows:

Genesis	Tobit [Tobias]	Baruch
Exodus	Judith	Ezekiel
Leviticus	Esther	Daniel
Numbers	1 Maccabees	Hosea [Osee]
Deuteronomy	2 Maccabees	Joel
Joshua	Job	Amos
Judges	Psalms	Obadiah [Abdias]
Ruth	Proverbs	Jonah
1 Samuel [1 Kings]	Ecclesiastes	Micah
2 Samuel [2 Kings]	Song of Songs	Nahum
1 Kings [3 Kings]	[Canticle of	
2 Kings [4 Kings]	Canticles]	Habakkuk
1 Chronicles	Wisdom	Zephaniah
[1 Paralipomenon]	Sirach	[Sophinias]
2 Chronicles	[Ecclesiasticus]	Haggai [Aggeus]
[2 Paralipomenon]	Isaiah	Zechariah
Ezra [Esdras]	Jeremiah	[Zacharias]
Nehemiah	Lamentations	Malachi
[Nehemias]		

Some of the books have an additional name listed in brackets. If you have a version of the Bible that is old enough, you may find that the names in brackets are used instead of the first name listed. There are forty-six books in the Old Testament.

While all forty-six of these books are considered to be inspired and part of Sacred Scripture by the Catholic Church, not all Christian churches accept this entire list. Many Christian churches that are not Catholic fail to agree with the conclusion that all forty-six books are inspired. Bibles used in Christian but non-Catholic traditions would often not include the following Old Testament books:

Tobit

Judith

Wisdom

Sirach

Baruch

1 Maccabees

2 Maccabees

Part of the Books of Daniel and Esther

The names of the New Testament books are as follows:

Gospel of Matthew	Ephesians	Hebrews
Gospel of Mark	Philippians	James
Gospel of Luke	Colossians	1 Peter
Gospel of John	1 Thessalonians	2 Peter
Acts of the Apostles	2 Thessalonians	1 John
Romans	1 Timothy	2 John
1 Corinthians	2 Timothy	3 John
2 Corinthians	Titus	Jude
Galatians	Philemon	Revelation

There are twenty-seven books of the New Testament. All Christian churches recognize each of these twenty-seven books as being part of the Bible.

In the New Testament list the letters from James through Jude are titled *from whom* they are sent. However, the letters beginning with Romans through Hebrews are titled according *to whom* they are sent. Many of these letters were originally addressed to people that lived in a specific area: Romans refers to the city of Rome in Italy, Corinthians refers to the city of Corinth in Greece, Galatians refers to the region of Galatia in Turkey, Ephesians refers to the city of Ephesus in Turkey, Philippians refers to the city of Philippi in Greece/Macedonia, Colossians refers to the city of Colossae in Turkey, Thessalonians refers to the city of Thessalonica in Greece/Macedonia, Hebrews refers to Jewish converts to Christ in an unspecified area.

We use the word "book" to designate each of the above. They were written at different times and many of them by different people. However, some of these "books" are as short as only a single page.

The listing above which matches the order of books found in the Bible is not a chronological listing. The books were not preserved in the order in which they were written. Even though the first book of the Bible, the book of Genesis, begins with the account of creation, the books do not continue in a historical sequence. The collectors were more interested in arranging the books according to the type of writing they contained.

Apocryphal Books

Sometimes in advertisements and introductions to the Bible, the words "apocrypha" or "apocryphal" are used. These words are used in one sense within the Catholic tradition, and in a different sense within the Protestant tradition.

When used within the Catholic religion the term "apocryphal books" refers to books that might deal with topics similar to those found in the Bible, but the books are not inspired and therefore not part of Sacred Scripture. There are about two thousand pages of New Testament apocrypha. Among the books in this category are titles like the Gospel of Judas Iscariot, the Gospel of Truth, the Gospel of Thomas, 3 Corinthians, and the Apocalypse of Thomas.

Within many Protestant traditions, however, the word "apocryphal" refers instead to those seven books that are not accepted by them as part of the Old Testament. These books are listed above on page 2. To make matters confusing, these seven books referred to by many Protestant traditions as "apocrypha" are referred to in the Catholic tradition as "deuterocanonical books."

And so, an advertisement by a Catholic publishing house indicating that a version of the Bible contains "deuterocanonical books" tells the reader that this particular version of the Bible contains the thirty-nine books of the Old Testament recognized by all Jewish and Christian traditions as well as the seven books recognized only within the Catholic and Orthodox traditions.

Finding a Certain Passage

References to the Bible begin with the most general category (the name of the book) and then narrow the passage down to the chapter and then the verse. The first word or group of words tells you the title of the book of the Bible. Practice will help you to know whether you can find this book in the Old Testament or New Testament, and approximately where in each group the book is located. If you are unsure as to where to look in your Bible to find a passage, most Bibles have a table of contents that will tell you the page number on which that book begins.

Depending on which version of the Bible you use, there are two different ways the page numbers can be listed. Some versions of the Bible begin with the first page of the Old Testament labeled page 1 and continue numbering as any other book would one page after the other, through the last page of the New Testament. Other Bibles start the Old Testament with page 1, and then start over with the New Testament on page 1. Being aware of the numbering method used by your particular Bible will help you to locate passages more easily.

When looking up Bible references also pay attention to any numbers in front of the book name. For example, 2 John refers to the second letter of John, while the name John by itself refers to the gospel.

The first number after the title tells you the chapter number of the book. These are easily found, as they are the largest numbers that appear throughout a book. The numbers that follow the colon refer to the verse numbers, which are the smaller numbers spread throughout the text.

Here are some sample references along with what they mean:

Genesis 1:1: the book of Genesis, chapter 1, verse 1

Genesis 1:1-10: the book of Genesis, chapter 1, verses 1 through 10

Genesis 1:1-10, 14: the book of Genesis, chapter 1, verses 1 through 10 and verse 14

Genesis 1:1–2:3: the book of Genesis, chapter 1, verse 1, through chapter 2, verse 3

As you look at a page in your Bible, any numbers or letters that are smaller in size than the verse numbers are references to footnotes.

Translations

Since the original language of the Scriptures is not English, the books of the Bible have been translated. To translate the Bible is a tremendous task which is not done frequently. However, from time to time, translations have been made to help bring the words of the original languages found in the Scriptures (Greek and Hebrew) to life for any given culture. Once a translation is completed, it is given a name. Some of the names of English translations and the dates when they were completed are: King James (1611), American Standard (1901), Revised Standard (1946), New English Bible (1961), Jerusalem Bible (1966), New American Bible (1970), New International Bible (1978), Bible in Today's English (1978), New Jerusalem Bible (1985), Revised New Testament of the New American Bible (1986), Revised English Bible (1989), New Revised Standard Version (1990).

To offer some idea of how translations differ, this is Luke 15:1 as found in six different translations:

> Then drew near unto him all the publicans and sinners for to hear him.
>
> —King James Translation

> One time many tax collectors and outcasts came to listen to Jesus.
>
> —Today's English Translation

> Now the tax collectors and sinners were all drawing near to him.
>
> —Revised Standard Translation

> One day when many tax collectors and other outcasts came to listen to Jesus . . .
>
> —Good News Translation

> The tax collectors and sinners were all gathering around to hear him.
>
> —New American Bible Translation

> The tax collectors and sinners were all drawing near to listen to him . . .
>
> —Revised New Testament of the New American Bible Translation

Currently the process of translating involves going back and making use of earlier texts that are in Hebrew and Greek. From this fact alone you can see that not many people are qualified to translate the Bible. Some translations can be geared to a particular reading audience, for example younger readers. Other translations can be done with the idea that they will be read out loud in public ceremonies. These may be done to address a wider audience than children. Either way, translations that are done from Hebrew and Greek are trying to be faithful to the earliest most accurate documents that are available. This is important, as what is being translated is God's Word, which when first written down was not put in English. It is to God's Word that the translator must be faithful.

There are two main approaches to translating the Bible. One is called "formal equivalence." This results in an almost "word for word" more literal translation. Another is called "dynamic equivalence." This approach is more dynamic and free in its effort to translate from one language to another. Sometimes this second approach can be *very* free to where the translator omits sections and takes a greater liberty in choosing words. This is known as a paraphrase. In a paraphrase, changes in the text can be considerable from what you would read in a translated Bible.

Have you ever gotten a page that had been photocopied so often that it was no longer as clear as the original? The further you get from an original, the less clear something can become. That is how it is with the Bible. The further someone gets from using the original languages of the Bible, the less like the original is the result. While a paraphrased Bible may be a helpful way to introduce a child to Scripture, a Bible that offers a translation will be much closer to the original language of the Scriptures.

Within the Catholic Church, the current translations that are most often used in our liturgies are the New American Bible (1970) for Old Testament texts and the Revised New Testament of the New American Bible (1986) for New Testament texts. Both of these can readily be found in one Bible.

Title Page

One of the first pages of the Bible, the title page, will contain much of the information you need to help choose the best Bible for your needs. The title page will indicate whether the Bible is a translation or a paraphrase. It also gives the name of the translation. For example, a title page with the words "New American Bible" indicates that the translation is the New American Bible translation.

One translation of the Bible can be published in several editions. Many Bibles include additional information, such as maps, charts, footnotes, introductions to each book, or a glossary. Any particular combination of these "extras" will make up a particular "edition." For example, the "Saint Joseph Edition of the New American Bible" uses all of the above additions so that those who would like can have more detail about what they are reading. There are other editions of the New American Bible. These contain the same translation, but a different set of "extras."

The title page will also indicate the type of texts upon which the translation depended. The phrase "translated from the original languages" denotes that the English was translated directly from the original Hebrew or Greek.

On the reverse of the title page, the word "imprimatur" indicates that the version of the Bible contains all seventy-three books of the Bible used within the Catholic tradition. This would include the seven books not accepted by some other Christian traditions.

Any translation with an imprimatur is certainly acceptable for any Catholic to use. Which translation or edition you read is a matter of your own preference. Select a translation that you are comfortable using. The words the translators use, and the organization of the Bible, and the "extras" it comes with are elements you will look at to make a decision.

Most Bibles, like most books, have a preface. Sometimes it is helpful to read the preface of the Bible. This will give more detailed information on what the translators had in mind when they did their work.

Chapter 2

Consider

Once you have a Bible, what comes next? Somehow it needs not only to be read, but understood. Our starting point turns now to this question: Should the Bible even be interpreted?

Interpretation involves looking at the Bible in a search for its meaning. There is a presumption behind the idea that something can be interpreted. That presumption can be worded this way: Sometimes there can be a difference between what is said (read, heard, seen) and what is meant. In other words, knowing what the Bible says is not always the same as understanding what the Bible means.

The skill of interpreting involves in part trying to determine whether or not these two things (what is said and what is meant) are identical in a given passage. Is what I read in a particular Bible passage identical to what is meant? If these two are not identical, then what exactly is being said? Answering these questions is a part of what it means to interpret.

Just looking at it from this point of view, not all religions or groups or individuals believe that the Bible should be interpreted. There are those who would have as their frame of reference that the Bible always and only means exactly what it says. There is no need to interpret Scripture. You read the words. What they say is identical to what they mean, at all times. Those who use this approach to understanding the Bible might not have much interest in what is suggested here.

The Catholic Church's point of view is that interpreting is a necessary step in understanding the words of Scripture. Having said this, it should be acknowledged that this is a more time consuming and challenging approach than one that says interpretation is not needed. That may be one of the reasons why it is an approach not always accepted by readers of the Bible.

Since there are different points of view about this basic question, let's first explore the basis for the Catholic Church seeing a need to interpret God's Word.

I would suggest that in order to get through life, the art and skill of interpreting is used consistently by most people, regardless of their religious affiliation. We are regularly interpreting the reality that comes through our senses.

Consider this example. Walter and Diane meet each other at work. They find themselves getting along well and enjoying each other's company. One day while Diane is at home the doorbell rings and a dozen roses are delivered. Diane quickly find herself thinking how thoughtful Walter is, and how anxious she is to see him again.

Now look at a different couple. Jack and Karen meet each other at work. They find themselves getting along and enjoying each other's company. One day while Karen is at home, the doorbell rings and a dozen roses are delivered. Sound similar? But now the ending is different. Karen quickly finds herself wondering, "What does he want from me? Why did he do this?" She becomes suspicious, and decides when they talk again, she'll have to be more guarded in how she acts.

In this example, the same event triggers two very different responses. How can this be? What explains the same event getting a different reaction?

Let's look at the example more closely. What is it that triggered the emotional response? Whether suspicion or joy, what led to that reaction? At first it might seem that the event did. Karen and Diane open the door, see the flowers, and react. Some might conclude the event triggered the response. But if that is all there is to it, then how do we explain two different reactions to the same event? It would seem there is a third part to this puzzle. There is apparently more to it than an event bringing about a response.

The missing piece is interpretation. After the event (Karen and Diane see the flowers) but before the reaction (suspicion or joy), something takes place. The action of being handed a dozen roses is interpreted. This occurs so quickly in most people that often times the individual is not aware it is happening.

So the actual process goes something like this:

1. There is an event.
2. From the event my mind comes up with an interpretation.
3. From how I interpret the event (not the event itself) flows my reaction.

We are regularly interpreting how others act. This is what allows different people to respond to the same event in different ways. We come up with different interpretations and therefore can have different reactions. Interpretation is built into our human nature. We are supposed to interpret how others act so that we can better understand the reality around us.

Not only do we interpret how people act, we also interpret what we read. For example:

> In sitting down paging through the newspaper, we read an editorial. Whether we agree or disagree with the author's point of view, we know up front that what we are reading is an opinion, not fact.

> Our approach to reading a factual account of a crime, however, would be different. Here we interpret what we are reading to be objectively accurate, unlike the opinion offered in the editorial. Our mind quickly changes the basis for how it interprets what we read. This is exactly as it should be.

> Next we turn to the movie section, and see the claim "Brilliant!" describing a new film release. However, even though we read that word we know the movie may not be as brilliant as the reviewer says.

> When we look at the weather report and see that it is not supposed to rain tomorrow, we won't be all that surprised if it does.

> When we read in a death notice that the deceased, Bob, was the "beloved" husband of Christine, we might interpret that more realistically if we knew the couple and were aware they didn't get along. In that case our mind would recognize the use of the word "beloved" as more part of a standard format in a death notice, rather than a genuine term of affection.

These changes in what our mind tells us about what we are reading occur so quickly we are often unaware that they even happen. Interpretation is built into our human nature. We are supposed to interpret what we read. This is exactly as it should be.

We also interpret what we hear. This is most obviously true when we hear figures of speech used. "My feet are killing me" doesn't mean exactly what it says. No one who understands English would hear that phrase and take it literally. Our mind quickly interprets those words. Who would take the statement "I have butterflies in my stomach" literally?

Have you ever been at a restaurant where most of the tables were full and you observed how busy it was? As you are seated the waiter comes to your table and says, "I'll be back in a minute." Your mind interprets that as it will probably be more than sixty seconds.

We also interpret what we see. You are driving at night and in the distance you see some kind of vehicle on the road with a single light moving in your direction. Your mind will interpret what you see. You may tell yourself it is a motorcycle or a car with one of its headlights out. How you decide to interpret what you see will also have something to do with how you act. If you think it may be a car without a headlight, not knowing which headlight is out, you may drive more closely to the curb, not knowing for sure if the approaching car is too close to your lane.

Dean and Anne are in different homes but watching the same show on TV. There is a scene of a patient in an intensive care unit. Anne is a nurse. She puts down the TV guide and becomes interested in the scene. As a nurse, she is wondering how the show will portray her profession. She watches intently. Then there's the other viewer. Dean has recently buried his father, who had been in an intensive care unit for several weeks before he died. As Dean watches the hospital scene it becomes all too real, and painful memories return. He immediately changes the channel. Both of them saw the same thing, but it meant something different to each of them. Their reactions (interest and anxiety) came from how they interpreted what they saw.

I would suggest that a basis for accepting the approach that the Bible should be open to interpretation is the conclusion that the need for interpreting is built into the world around us. We interpret what we read, see, hear, and how others act. This is as it should be. Interpreting helps us to make sense out of the world. Does it make sense that the Bible should be the only thing that is not open to interpretation? The necessity of interpreting is even more evident when we consider the historical and cultural context in which the sacred books were written, and how these differ from our own today.

One of the challenges of interpreting Scripture is to open God's Word to as much meaning as possible, but in a way that what is interpreted corresponds to a message God wants us to receive. Does it seem reasonable to always limit that meaning by proposing that everything in the Bible always means exactly what it says? If this does not work with the rest of reality, why should it work with Scripture? This is not a weakness in life, but rather helps bring about a fuller meaning of what is around us. Even Jesus did not speak literally all the time.

Being able to interpret the Bible is what helps explain five people coming up with five different interpretations—while at the same time remaining consistent with the rest of Scripture. It allows for various homilies to be preached on a weekend that don't all say the same thing over and over. This helps make this collection of sacred books meaningful for people of each new generation who read it. This approach should encourage each person to find meaning in his or her life through these words.

Having said this, we now need to address another part of the question: Are the interpretations we come up with always accurate? Because we arrive at a certain conclusion, does that always mean that is the same as what God might be trying to tell us? In other words, can we make a mistake in interpreting? Let's consider some examples:

> Stephanie is a high school junior. She gets above average grades. She accepts additional responsibilities that support her high school community. Stephanie is a popular person who is known for her friendly smile. Teachers, friends, and even parents often "interpret" her smile as an indication that life is going well for her. However, that interpretation has been based on externals. In fact, it is possible that she is unhappy and has the same range of problems that anyone else her age has. A smile and good grades should not always be interpreted as a lack of problems and a feeling of happiness. To do so in some cases would be to interpret falsely. Some people smile precisely in order to prevent people from seeing the reality.

> Driving down a street you see an elderly man walking on the sidewalk in an uneven pattern. Your mind might interpret what you see as an example of someone who has been drinking. What if in reality the gentleman has Alzheimer's and he can no longer walk in a steady manner? Your initial interpretation would be inaccurate.

> You walk into a room of people you have never seen before. As you look around the room you begin to interpret what you see. One individual gets your attention and without knowing anything about the person your mind interprets that individual's appearance as being someone you'd like to get to know better. You see someone else and you decide that during the break you'll avoid that person. What if your interpretations were all false? In the process of preparing couples for marriage sometimes I'll ask them what they thought of each other when they first met. It's not uncommon to hear people say that when they first met, one didn't care for the other . . . and yet eventually they decide to marry. It can be easy for us to misinterpret at first.

We can certainly misinterpret what we read, see, hear, and how others act. What accounts for our ability to misinterpret the reality around us? I'll offer one possibility by way of an analogy.

John lives six miles from work. Every day he drives the same set of roads to get there from his home. He travels on four different streets. He turns at the same intersections each day, drives on the same roads, and arrives at about the same time. He has traveled this route so often that he feels he could do it in his sleep. Sometimes if he is tired or preoccupied during his drive he finds that suddenly he has arrived at work, and almost wonders to himself, "How did I get here?" He might not even remember making the normal turns or stopping at the usual lights. He had become so accustomed to traveling one particular route that it just became second nature after a while.

I think there is a sense in which this can apply to how our mind works as well. Whenever we interpret the world around us, we can become accustomed to thinking in certain ways and interpreting using a familiar path. Have you ever met people who seemed to "collect" holding grudges? Whatever happens in life is filtered through their mind telling them that what they experience is being done on purpose to hurt them. People who feel this way will interpret what they see and hear through this familiar path they have "traveled" over and over. It can happen automatically, without even thinking about it. People who do this fail to realize that not everyone they see or everything they read or hear fits that common way of interpreting that their mind has become comfortable with.

How we interpret the world around us is influenced by many factors: how we were raised, the friends with whom we associate, traumatic experiences, even the condition of our own health can influence the patterns of how we interpret the world around us. These influences have the ability to prejudice the conclusions we come to in this process of interpreting.

Although interpretation is a part of how we deal with the reality around us, there is a certain skill in doing it well. Probably all of us can recall a time when we were on the receiving end of someone misinterpreting something we had said or done. We all know misinterpretation can occur.

Let's take this idea and apply it to the Bible. If we can interpret other things around us inaccurately, can we do the same with the Bible? To me, this seems as obvious as all the other areas of life . . . yes, we can interpret the Bible wrongly.

Let me offer some examples of what to me seem like flawed interpretations of the Bible:

> I remember once listening to a worship service on the radio where the person preaching was talking about the rainbow that appeared in the sky after the flood during Noah's time. The minister was describing what a rainbow looked like and the different colors that you could see. However, he eventually interpreted that event as being an indication from God that the races should not inhabit the same land together. The preacher proceeded to say that since the colors in a rainbow are distinguished enough that you can tell the separate colors, that this is God's way of telling us that the different colors found in the races should live in distinct areas as well. There should be separate countries for each race. The Catholic Church's approach to Scripture would prohibit that kind of an interpretation. We would consider it an incorrect use of the Bible.

> A health food store distributed a written advertisement for a certain brand of bee pollen capsules, which the manufacturer suggests be taken as a food supplement. It carries with it references to certain passages of the Bible that speak of honey. The advertisement indicates that "honey bee pollen is God's chosen food," and that it is God who to this day com-

mands us to eat it. Using passages in that way to promote the necessity of consuming bee pollen is an inaccurate way to interpret Scripture.

A community in the northeast part of the country had formed what they referred to as a church commune. The state was concerned about reports of physical and psychological abuse that were occurring to the children there. The leadership of the commune attempted to justify the children being spanked and beaten by quoting from the Psalms, "Serve the LORD with fear" (Ps 2:11). Such a passage is used inaccurately when its purpose is to defend that kind of discipline.

"When someone strikes you on [your] right cheek, turn the other one to him as well" (Matt 5:39). That cannot be used to demonstrate that domestic violence is somehow a lifestyle that must be tolerated and lived with.

In the translation of the New American Bible, the word "healer" is used only two times. In both instances the healer is God. From time to time we hear about different sects that conclude that all healing comes directly from God alone. Therefore, if someone is seriously ill, they take the position that the person should just stay at home and be prayed over, until God decides to heal or wants the person to die. After all, they see in the words of Scripture that it is neither physicians nor medicine that brings about a cure, but only God. Is this what God is trying to tell us by these kinds of passages?

Some cults have been known to use the Bible to help justify the behaviors they ask of their membership. "If anyone comes to me without hating his father and mother, wife and children, brothers and sisters, and even his own life, he cannot be my disciple" (Luke 14:26). A television program on cults showed an interview with a young man who had been "rescued" from a cult he had participated in for years. In it, he said this was the quote that those in the cult used to help lure him into the group. They told him that in the Bible it is God who encourages us to leave our families behind and give up contact with them. Therefore, he was told, the secrecy a cult provides is all part of God's plan. Does that seem to be an authentic use of Scripture?

"Do you think that I have come to establish peace on the earth? No, I tell you, but rather division" (Luke 12:51). Since God has come to bring division, then isn't that our job as well? Shouldn't we do whatever we feel is necessary, even if conflict results? A man who set a bomb in an abortion clinic used this same passage to justify what he did. Was he acting in accord with Scripture?

Consider the Scripture passage that describes the Baptism of Jesus. Suppose someone interprets that to mean that since Jesus was baptized when he was an adult, children and babies should never be baptized. Such a person might conclude that Jesus' adult baptism means that anyone who chooses baptism should do so only as an adult. At least within the Catholic tradition we have not found this to be an authentic way to interpret such a passage.

A woman was interviewed last year during a news segment entitled "alternative lifestyles." She belonged to a group of couples who believed that within marriage, infidelity was an acceptable practice and was to be encouraged. During the program, the interviewer asked, "How do you respond to those who disagree with what you do?" Her answer was to quote Scripture, "Stop judging and you will not be judged" (Luke 6:37). Do you think Jesus meant this command to help people justify practices that he himself condemned?

These examples are meant to show that the Bible, like other things and events, can be interpreted incorrectly. Passages in the Bible can be used in ways that God never intended. Even Hitler quoted Scripture in some of his speeches to justify what he wanted done.

There must be some objective way we can determine if how we interpret the Bible is consistent with what God wants us to receive. So far I am suggesting that Scripture, like most things, needs to be interpreted. However, like everything else, we can use it in a way that is not authentic. Now we turn to the next question: How do we know if we are interpreting correctly? To begin to answer this question I'll suggest an analogy starting with some examples that are not from the Bible.

Allow yourself to interpret what you see in this picture. Don't ask yourself what you see, but rather reflect on what it means. When you look at it, what does it communicate to you? What does it make you think about? Before reading further, in the box below write one sentence beginning with the word "I" that reflects an idea you have when you see this picture.

I

While there are many possible responses, let's consider these three:

1. I remember what a happy day my wedding was.
2. I need to get a gift; our anniversary is next week.
3. I know I'm married, but I'm going to continue the affair.

Society has no problem with the first two interpretations. Even though they are different interpretations, both are equally acceptable. If we were to visualize this, we could use a circle. The numbers below refer to the three statements above.

Inside the circle there is room for numerous interpretations of what the picture represents—a marriage. We could locate the first and second interpretations inside the circle. However, the third one is in a different category. To show this, the third interpretation is located outside the circle. To be sure, some people would relate to the third interpretation, but it is not one that many people would encourage. It is not one that supports the picture of two hands united and a promise made. Even the Scriptures speak of the fidelity of one spouse to another. Interpretations can be placed inside or outside of the circle, to show whether they are somehow flawed.

Let's go on to another example. Consider this picture:

As before, how do you interpret what this picture represents? Come up with a sentence beginning with the word "I" that reflects an idea you have when you see this picture, and write it below. What does it communicate to you?

I

Here are samples of what others may have written:

1. I miss my mother who died last year.
2. I wish I could leave all my problems behind; suicide is the answer.
3. I'll go to the cemetery next week to clean off my grandfather's grave.

Interpretations one and three have something in common, which separates them from the second. The second one is in a different category—it is an option most of us would not encourage. We could visualize these various interpretations in this way:

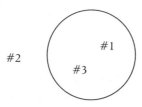

Let's go onto a third example, following this same pattern.

Write your sentence here:

I

What are some possible interpretations?

1. I know this hospital performs abortions. I'm going to place a bomb in the emergency room.

2. I remember giving birth there. Seeing the picture gives me a feeling of joy.

3. I feel sad when I drive past the hospital. My father died there.

First, notice how the second and third interpretations are almost opposite. One talks of joy and the other of sadness. Just as the same picture can be interpreted in very different ways, so can the same passage from Scripture. Because the same verse from the Bible is interpreted differently by people does not mean one person has to be wrong. Interpretations do not always have to be identical in order to be acceptable. However, having said that, there are some interpretations that would cause concern to most people.

Consider the difference between the first interpretation and those numbered two and three. Society has decided that while we are free to express our views, we cannot do what the person in the first statement proposes. Here's how it can be visualized:

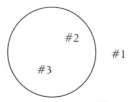

Looking at this picture, what is one way you might interpret what you see?

Write down your thought here:

I

Let's consider some additional possibilities:

1. I'm looking forward to my wedding there.
2. I should probably start to pray more often.
3. I think that religion is the source of all problems. I'm going to do something to destroy this building. (This is the actual conclusion an arsonist came to before he burned a church.)

The third interpretation is the one that causes concern. It is outside the circle of what is acceptable.

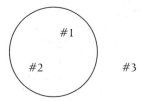

These examples are trying to demonstrate that there can be several different interpretations to any one thing we see. However, sometimes an interpretation can allow a person to believe or act in a way that will not be helpful.

I think this kind of approach, with a few adjustments, can be applied to Scripture. Many passages in the Bible have multiple meanings, but like everything else, if we're not careful we can reach an interpretation that is communicating something other than what God wants us to hear.

For Scripture we can use certain criteria to help give us an idea of when we are inside or outside the circle of what God may be trying to tell us. The guidelines offered in the next chapter will help us be able to tell the difference.

Chapter 3

Interpret

So far I have suggested that the Bible, like much of the reality around us, is able to be interpreted. This involves opening up the meaning of the Scriptures in as many ways as are authentic. Caution must be used, however, because just like other things we interpret, our conclusions as to what God is saying can be flawed. This chapter examines some guidelines that can be used to help keep us within the circle of a healthy and acceptable use of Scripture. They provide for us a way to know when we are outside of that circle, that is, when our interpretation would no longer seem likely to hold whatever God wants us to believe as coming from God.

In the Acts of the Apostles, the story is told of Philip meeting an official from Ethiopia. This official was an educated man, in charge of the treasury of the queen of the Ethiopians. He had come to Jerusalem to worship and was returning home when he met Philip. In this scene, the official is reading from the prophet Isaiah. Philip asks him, "Do you understand what you are reading?" He replies, "How can I, unless someone instructs me?" This chapter is meant to help serve that purpose.

The guidelines are offered to help us expand the ways in which we can look for the meaning of what we read. They are each followed by an explanation and some examples from the Bible.

Begin with Prayer

To interpret is to ask for God's help in making the Word evermore alive in our lives. It is a process of coming to understand and appreciate who Jesus is and how we fit into spreading his kingdom. Before we

21

begin, it is worthwhile to place ourselves before him as we ask for his guidance in making the Scriptures come alive. It provides us with a chance to renew once again our desire to be open to what he has to say. A prayer such as this might be a way to begin:

> Father, your love for us was so great
> that long ago your Word became flesh, and Jesus was born.
>
> You promised to be with us always.
> Your presence is the Eucharist and your voice is the Scripture.
>
> Encourage us to read your Word,
> for it is here we find your wisdom.
> Help us to think about your Word,
> for it is here we find your compassion and strength.
> Guide us to be changed by your Word,
> for it is here we find you.
>
> On the road to Emmaus, you opened the minds of your friends
> to the understanding of the Scriptures.
>
> Open my mind now,
> that I may more completely live my life in union with yours,
> and help spread your kingdom in my home, my parish, and our world.
>
> Grant this through Christ Our Lord. Amen.

The Context of a Passage Can Make Its Meaning More Clear

Driving down a road, you run across this sign:

> Road under construction
> Two miles

The sign can be interpreted in two ways. It means either *beginning with the sign* construction occurs for the next two miles, or two miles *after the sign* road construction begins.

How can you quickly tell which meaning is accurate? By looking around you for evidence of construction. No people working, no machinery, no cones on the road will tell you which of the two meanings is correct. If we want to interpret something correctly, it helps to look around.

A bumper sticker reads: "Some mornings I wake up grouchy." That might be interpreted to mean that the owner of the car does not particularly enjoy getting up in the morning. But the meaning completely changes if we read the second sentence. The actual bumper sticker reads: "Some mornings I wake up grouchy. Other mornings I let him sleep." Now the meaning has changed completely. The first sentence is not understood until the second sentence is read.

A sign on an office desk reads: "I'd like to help you out." That means one thing. But continuing the same sign adds: "Which way did you come in?" Notice how the meaning is actually the opposite of what you first read.

"Shoot first. Ask questions later." We've all heard those words before. But put the words on a sign, add a pair of dice, and place it outside a Las Vegas casino, and it takes on a whole different meaning.

These simple examples illustrate something we can apply to Scripture as well, but of course with a greater degree of seriousness. Sometimes we have to be careful and "look around" the passage we are reading to understand its meaning correctly. In other words, it can be helpful to read what comes before and after any verse we are trying to interpret. Let's consider some examples from the Bible.

> Rejoice, O young man, while you are young,
>   and let your heart be glad in the days of your youth.
> Follow the ways of your heart,
>   the vision of your eyes.
>
> —Ecclesiastes 11:9

If we read only those words and go no further, it would seem as if the Bible gives us the ability to do as we please and to "follow our heart" without restraint. This interpretation would seem to say that commandments or norms do not really contribute to the discussion of right and wrong. Instead, there is one thing that forms the basis for morality: what is in your heart. However, if we continue reading the very next verse, that notion would change. The verse continues: "Yet understand that as regards all this God will bring you to judgment." It is the second sentence that helps us to interpret the first verse more honestly.

> There is no God.
>   —Psalm 14:1

Even an atheist can use the Bible to prove his or her own lack of belief as being accurate. From this sentence, the Psalms seem to admit that this notion of God is made up. But that is true only if we fail to notice the phrase that comes before it: "The fool says in his heart . . . ." Sometimes reading the verse before and after helps us to get a better insight into what God is trying to tell us.

> Again, [amen,] I say to you, if two of you agree on earth about anything for which they are to pray, it shall be granted to them by my heavenly Father.
>
> —Matthew 18:19

Can this passage mean that whenever two people pray for anything, God will do it? I think the experience of most of us would recognize that does not happen. Whenever we gather to celebrate the Eucharist and we offer petitions, there are more than two people praying for each petition offered. Over the years at Mass we've all prayed for an end to violence, hatred, and famine. Yet, how many of these work out the way we have prayed for? Think about it: if we could pray for anything and have a guarantee that it would be carried out by God, then that would make us more powerful than God. God would be our servant and we would be God's master. It simply can't be this way. And yet, Jesus said it. So, what is one way it can be interpreted?

The words that follow give us some help for a possible interpretation: "For where two or three are gathered together in my name, there am I in the midst of them."

In this added verse there is no indication that God does whatever we say, but a promise that he will be with us. When we join the two passages together, perhaps God is assuring us of this: there will be times when our prayer helps bring about a particular need and other times when God will be with us to help us see the difficulty through, but it will not be removed. God acts in both ways. Having looked at both verses together helps us to understand.

> A wife does not have authority over her own body, but rather her husband [does].
>
> —1 Corinthians 7:4

This passage cannot be interpreted as God's call for blind obedience and control of one spouse over the other. We know this because the verse continues: "and similarly a husband does not have authority over his own body, but rather his wife [does]." When looked at as a whole the passage is more a statement about equality rather than domination. However, that's only seen if you keep reading.

Be Careful Not to Interpret in a Way that Contradicts What God Has Revealed about Himself

> Then James and John, the sons of Zebedee, came to him and said to him, "Teacher, we want you to do for us whatever we ask of you." He replied, "What do you wish [me] to do for you?" They answered him, "Grant that in your glory we may sit one at your right and the other at your left." Jesus said to them, "You do not know what you are asking. Can you drink the cup that I drink or be baptized with the same baptism with which I am baptized?" They said to him, "We can." Jesus said to them, "The cup that I drink you will drink, and with the baptism with which I am baptized, you will be baptized; but to sit at my right or at my left is not mine to give but is for those for whom it has been prepared."
>
> —Mark 10:35-40

Some people go through life with a sense that everything in their future is totally in the control of God, as if he has already decided every aspect of their life and for that matter, what will happen after they leave this world as well. It is all a forgone conclusion. We are simply walking through what has already been determined and have no control.

This notion of predestination might seem to be supported by the last verse of this passage: "to sit at my right or my left is not mine to give but is for those for whom it has been prepared." Yet such an interpretation would contradict one of the great beliefs about God—that he has given us freedom. It would not be a correct use of Scripture to quote this last verse as an indication that God is telling us that our lives are predestined and we can do nothing to change that. Such an interpretation would be outside the circle of what is authentic, as it contradicts revealed truths about God. For while he certainly knows our future, the knowledge that God possesses is not what controls us. God does give us freedom to a significant degree.

> And how could a thing remain, unless you willed it;
>   or be preserved, had it not been called forth by you?
> But you spare all things, because they
>   are yours, O LORD and lover of souls,
> for your imperishable spirit is in all things!
>
> —Wisdom 11:25–12:1

Most of us would agree that there is a value in protecting our planet and in being careful about the resources that we use. The passage above might even be used to help support such an idea from a biblical point of view. However, if someone was going to interpret "your imperishable spirit is in all things" as a way of saying that human beings, plants, animals—anything found in creation—is of equal value, that would not be a proper interpretation of that passage. I remember watching a show on animal care and hearing the speaker come to this conclusion: "A bird with a wounded wing has the same right to life as a human being in a wheel chair." Such a conclusion could not be reached from this passage. One of the things we know about God from the story of creation in Genesis and other passages is the fact that there is something special and unique about life created in God's image and likeness—human beings. However the passage is interpreted, it cannot contradict that revelation.

> For I, the LORD, your God, am a jealous God, inflicting punishments for their fathers' wickedness on the children of those who hate me, down to the third and fourth generation but bestowing mercy, down to the thousandth generation, on the children of those who love me and keep my commandments.
>
> —Deuteronomy 5:9-10

How many people still think that when something has gone wrong in their life it is automatically because God is punishing them for something they have done? This passage takes it a step further and on the surface would suggest that God will do this not only to you, but to the next three or four generations after you! To take this passage and use it as a way to convince yourself or others that misfortune is to be seen as a punishment from God because of what you have done makes God out to be as petty and revengeful as we can be. God has revealed something different about himself, as seen in this passage:

> The son shall not be charged with the guilt of his father, nor shall the father be charged with the guilt of his son. The virtuous man's virtue shall be his own, as the wicked man's wickedness shall be his own.
>
> —Ezekiel 18:20

Caution: This guideline provides us with an example of how carefully these principles need to be used. This principle and all the ones that follow in this chapter are meant to be looked at as a whole, rather than individually. Once all the principles are considered, then the interpretation we make is more likely to be an accurate one.

For example, we have just considered the idea that we cannot interpret a passage in a way that contradicts what God has revealed about himself. In applying this guideline, one person might make the case for saying since the first quote from Deuteronomy contains the idea that God does punish one generation after the other, but then the quote from Ezekiel reveals something different about the hand of God, that the interpretation should be consistent with showing the mercy of God. But another person might take the opposite approach. Since the mercy of God as seen in Ezekiel's quote is contradicted by Deuteronomy, then the less merciful interpretation is accurate.

The key here is not to use each of the principles in this chapter individually, but rather collectively. There is a sense in which we are called to interpret the Bible, rather than just an individual passage. Once the guidelines in this chapter are looked at together, then the ways to interpret become clearer.

When Two Passages Seem to Contradict Each Other, Instead of an "Either . . . or" Interpretation, Try a "Both . . . and" Interpretation

This guideline is a reminder that individual passages of Scriptures should always be interpreted by the rest of Scripture. If two verses seem to be saying something different, look for truth in both of them, rather than just one. Many parts of the Bible have what might be called a "companion verse" that helps to determine the meaning of the passage:

> When the just cry out the LORD hears
> and rescues them from all distress.
>
> —Psalm 34:18

Let's consider the example of a person diagnosed with cancer. This individual reading the above passage sincerely cries out to the Lord asking to be cured. The cancer patient looks for what the psalmist promises: freedom from all distress. Should the cancer progress, then questions arise: "Where is God? Was I lied to? Should I continue to believe? Did I pray hard enough?" The reality is, there are other passages in the Bible that have something to say about how God deals with us:

> . . . and whoever does not take up his cross and follow after me is not worthy of me.
>
> —Matthew 10:38

As we come to interpret God's role in suffering, we do not have to accept only one of the above approaches. God has revealed that both of them have something to do with getting through life. God does much to help us, but again we cannot control God. All the difficulties of our life will not vanish because we pray for them to go away. For some aspects of our life we must take up our cross. It isn't that one or the other passage is true, it is that they both are.

Look at the birds in the sky; they do not sow or reap, they gather nothing into barns, yet your heavenly Father feeds them. Are you not more important than they? Can any of you by worrying add a single moment to your life-span? Why are you anxious about clothes? Learn from the way the wild flowers grow. They do not work or spin. But I tell you that not even Solomon in all his splendor was clothed like one of them. If God so clothes the grass of the field, which grows today and is thrown into the oven tomorrow, will he not much more provide for you, O you of little faith? So do not worry and say, "What are we to eat?" or "What are we to drink?" or "What are we to wear?"

—Matthew 6:26-31

The interpretation seems obvious: don't worry about what will sustain your life, because God will provide. But that interpretation raises some questions. Why do we send missionaries to help others in providing for the very needs God says not to worry about? Why do we take up collections to help others in want? Why does a Saint Vincent de Paul Society collect blankets and clothing? After all, we are told not to worry about such things. It is in part because other passages in the Bible have something to add. For example:

Or what king marching into battle would not first sit down and decide whether with ten thousand troops he can successfully oppose another king advancing upon him with twenty thousand troops? But if not, while he is still far away, he will send a delegation to ask for peace terms.

—Luke 14:31-32

Here the message is different: worry about sustaining your life . . . plan . . . don't expect God to figure it all out for you. Instead of interpreting one passage without benefit of the other, we can look at them together. Sometimes things are worth worrying about, other times they are not. This may not seem like much of a revelation, unless of course a person does only one or the other: worries about everything or about nothing.

> [But] take care not to perform righteous deeds in order that people may see them; otherwise, you will have no recompense from your heavenly Father.
>
> —Matthew 6:1

This passage cautions us about doing things solely for the purpose of showing others how generous we are. But we have to be careful not to take this to extremes. It wouldn't be a helpful interpretation for someone to use this passage to justify their unwillingness to help out with something needed at the parish. A passage from the previous chapter of this same book adds this idea:

> Just so, your light must shine before others, that they may see your good deeds and glorify your heavenly Father.
>
> —Matthew 5:16

There are times when we are called to act in the sight of others. The best interpretation of passages such as these occurs when we come up with a statement that includes both of these ideas together. We are all called to serve. However, we do this not to win the approval of others, but more with the idea that if others see what is done, it may offer them the encouragement they need to step forward and join in building up God's kingdom.

> But when you pray, go to your inner room, close the door, and pray to your Father in secret. And your Father who sees in secret will repay you.
>
> —Matthew 6:6

This passage seen by itself would suggest there is no need for public worship. Here we are told that when we pray it is to be in private. So why do we have to go to church each weekend? In part it is because passages in Scripture give further directions on how to pray:

> For where two or three are gathered together in my name, there am I in the midst of them.
>
> —Matthew 18:20

Here a different aspect of prayer is offered. God is with us when there is more than one, when we are not alone. The best interpretation of this is not to look solely at one or the other verse, but at both passages. God may be reminding us that both private and public prayer are essential for the Christian.

⁓

> I no longer call you slaves, because a slave does not know what his master is doing. I have called you friends, because I have told you everything I have heard from my Father.
>
> —John 15:15

It is an honor to be called a friend of God, as Jesus tells us we are. And yet, if we interpret this as somehow being God's equal or as not being bound by any law, then we have forgotten there are other passages in Scripture. In one passage, Jesus qualifies who his friends are:

> You are my friends if you do what I command you.
>
> —John 15:14

In another verse he refers to us in a different way altogether:

> Who among you would say to your servant who has just come in from plowing or tending sheep in the field, "Come here immediately and take your place at table"? Would he not rather say to him, "Prepare something for me to eat. Put on your apron and wait on me while I eat and drink. You may eat and drink when I am finished"? Is he grateful to that servant because he did what was commanded? So should it be with you. When you have done all you have been commanded, say, "We are unprofitable servants; we have done what we were obliged to do."
>
> —Luke 17:7-10

The notion that true followers of Jesus are servants is repeated in John's Gospel:

> Whoever serves me must follow me, and where I am, there also will my servant be. The Father will honor whoever serves me.
>
> —John 12:26

Even Saint Paul includes the challenge:

> Whatever you do, do from the heart, as for the Lord and not for others, knowing that you will receive from the Lord the due payment of the inheritance; be slaves of the Lord Christ.
>
> —Colossians 3:23

So, are we servants or friends? Instead of looking at one passage without the other, we can see truth in all of them. We can have a special relationship with God, but we are not God's equal.

Religion that is pure and undefiled before God and the Father is this: to care for orphans and widows in their affliction and to keep oneself unstained by the world.

—James 1:27

It is possible for people to conclude that because of the good things they do and the fact that they are generous in the way they help others, that they do not need to go to church and pray. An individual might feel little need for prayer, as he or she is already a "good person." Taken to more of an extreme, some might even be critical of those who go to church on the weekend and pray. After all, this passage stresses the importance of being good to people, and says nothing about the necessity of prayer. But there are other passages that add to the responsibilities of a Christian:

With all prayer and supplication, pray at every opportunity in the Spirit.

—Ephesians 6:18

This passage as well as others in Scripture tell us there is more to being a Christian than "being nice" to people. In reality, it is certainly possible to be genuinely interested in the welfare of others, while not even having a belief in God. To understand the responsibilities of a Christian, we look at all passages like these together rather than separately. A passage that combines both ideas is found in Mark's Gospel:

"Which is the first of all the commandments?" Jesus replied, "The first is this: 'Hear, O Israel! The Lord our God is Lord alone! You shall love the Lord your God with all your heart, with all your soul, with all your mind and with all your strength.' The second is this: 'You shall love your neighbor as yourself.'"

—Mark 12:28-31

We can't use loving our neighbor as a substitute for loving our God.

> For, if you confess with your mouth that Jesus is Lord and believe in your heart that God raised him from the dead, you will be saved.
>
> —Romans 10:9

This passage emphasizes beliefs that are internal to the individual—the necessity of believing in the Resurrection, as well as the ability to put into words the belief that Jesus is Lord. A person might read this verse and interpret it to mean that all that is necessary for salvation is to believe in your mind that Jesus is Lord and that he was raised. But there is another side to one of the challenges of faith, which is seen more clearly in another passage:

> What good is it, my brothers, if someone says he has faith but does not have works?
>
> —James 2:14

This passage connects belief with how the Christian acts. By looking at the truth of both passages, we come to a clearer understanding of what is expected of us: belief as well as the practice of faith.

> Blessed are the peacemakers,
>   for they will be called children of God.
>
> —Matthew 5:9

On more than one occasion Jesus offers his peace. Sometimes it is in the form of a greeting, and other times he talks about what this gift means. Here, he encourages us to be peacemakers in the world. But Saint Luke records some other ideas about the role of peace:

> I have come to set the earth on fire, and how I wish it were already blazing! There is a baptism with which I must be baptized, and how great is my anguish until it is accomplished! Do you think that I have come to establish peace on the earth? No, I tell you, but rather division.
>
> —Luke 12:49-51

Perhaps we understand better when we combine both ideas. At times God brings us peace, and at times God shakes us up. Could both of these also be our role in how we deal with the world around us? Is our challenge in being followers of Christ only to keep the world at peace with how it operates and what it provides? Can't a person be a good Christian and at the same time fight for worthy causes?

> What man among you having a hundred sheep and losing one of them would not leave the ninety-nine in the desert and go after the lost one until he finds it? And when he does find it, he sets it on his shoulders with great joy and, upon his arrival home, he calls together his friends and neighbors and says to them, "Rejoice with me because I have found my lost sheep."
>
> —Luke 15:4-7

In the fifteenth chapter of Luke we are told the parables of the lost sheep, the lost coin and lost son. The stories are reminders to us of how God searches and helps bring back what is lost. But another passage of Scripture presents us with an added idea:

> Jesus said to them, "Amen, amen, I say to you, unless you eat the flesh of the son of Man and drink his blood, you do not have life within you." . . . Then many of his disciples who were listening said, "This saying is hard; who can accept it?" Since Jesus knew that his disciples were murmuring about this, he said to them, "Does this shock you? What if you were to see the Son of Man ascending to where he was before? It is the spirit that gives life, while the flesh is of no avail. The words I have spoken to you are spirit and life. But there are some of you who do not believe." Jesus knew from the beginning the ones who would not believe and the one who would betray him. And he said, "For this reason I have told you that no one can come to me unless it is granted him by my Father."
>
> As a result of this, many [of] his disciples returned to their former way of life and no longer accompanied him. Jesus then said to the Twelve, "Do you also want to leave?"
>
> —John 6:53, 60-67

In the Bread of Life discourse, Jesus speaks of the great gift of his body and blood to be shared. John tells us that his words were difficult to accept, and that "many" of those who heard them no longer accompanied Jesus. This passage gives no indication that Jesus goes after them. Unlike the lost sheep, coin, or son, he lets them go and asks the Twelve if they want to leave as well. To be sure, God does care for us when we stray. However, with the freedom we have we can stay lost if we choose.

Using this guideline can seem like a lot of work, because it means we have to be familiar with how one verse of Scripture is connected to another.

It raises the question: Why didn't Jesus just speak more plainly? When he talks about prayer for example, why didn't he present a more complete idea all at once? Perhaps the answer has to do with the audience he was talking to at the time.

For example, maybe on the occasion where Jesus was talking about going to your room and praying alone, these words were spoken to people who were very good at going to the temple on the Sabbath, but did not have much to do with God during the rest of the week. It would seem reasonable that at least at times Jesus would tailor his words so that his immediate audience would benefit. And so to them, he talks of the value of private prayer (going to your room and closing the door).

And then at some point he speaks with a different group who have come to value private prayer, but stay away from prayer with others. To them he talks about the value of common prayer (where two or three are gathered). This helps to explain why everything isn't always in one place in the Bible.

In practice using this guideline in interpreting Scripture is not always easy, as it requires something of a knowledge of what other passages say about a given topic. The more familiar we become with the Bible, the more accurately we can understand all of the revelations Jesus offers. However, you don't always have to depend on your own memory, thanks to a book called a concordance. This book gives an alphabetical listing of words used in the Bible, as well as the reference where each is located. So, if you want to know what Jesus says about "prayer," you will find a listing of each of the passages where that word is used. By looking them up, you will get a more complete idea of what God reveals. Not only is this kind of book available in print, but some publishing houses have made it available on CD-ROMs for use on a computer. Be careful though to make sure that the concordance you use is one that matches the translation of the Bible that you are reading.

The Bible Records a Development of Ideas

This is particularly important to keep in mind when we compare passages from the Old and New Testaments. One of the ideas we learn from the study of Scripture is that God has revealed himself gradually. This is evident in the Bible which from beginning to end took about thirteen centuries to write. God must have seen some advantages to a gradual revelation of himself.

A thunderstorm can bring down a great deal of rain for half an hour. Then it stops and the sun comes out. If you go outside and dig into the ground, you will find that not too far down the earth is perfectly dry. However, instead of a thunderstorm, let's say there is a gentle sprinkle of rain for a day. The same amount of rain falls as during the storm, but now when you dig into the earth it is soft and wet. The rain had the chance to sink in and was absorbed into the ground. God may have had this kind of advantage in mind as he revealed himself to us. A slower and gradual revelation would give us time to let things sink in. Maybe this is what was behind Jesus' occasional warning to people not to tell others about what they had seen (Matt 9:30; Mark 8:30, etc.). It may have been his way of slowing down the revelation about himself.

The Bible records ideas that are developing throughout the pages of Scripture. Understanding this process of revelation keeps us from just randomly opening the Bible to any passage and presuming that what we are reading is the fullest revelation of a particular idea. While it is true that we are still discovering God's call in Scripture, it is not uncommon that it is Jesus who provides a clearer development of a particular teaching.

Even in Jesus' teaching, he acknowledges that ideas are developing. For example, when the Pharisees ask him, "Is it lawful for a husband to divorce his wife?" Jesus replies by telling them what Moses allowed "because of the hardness of your hearts," and then proceeds to give them a new idea about what it means to be joined (Mark 10:1-9).

All of this certainly provides a challenge for the reader of Scripture. Are there further revelations in other books of the Bible about what I am reading? If this approach is followed in the Bible, then isn't much of the Bible inaccurate? If it isn't all true, then how do I know which parts to believe? These are important questions which church and tradition help answer. Let's consider an analogy to help understand this better.

Do you have an address book with the names, addresses, and phone numbers of friends or people you want to keep tract of? Over time though, some of these people move. They change their address and maybe their phone number as well. What do you do to your address book to reflect these changes? One possibility is you can put a line through an earlier address and then write in the new information at the end of the list of names for that page in the alphabet.

Over a span of years, the information you originally recorded for some of the individuals will never have changed at all. What you recorded about their location five years ago remains the same. Some of the other names will be crossed out and their current information will be listed further down the page.

One day you need someone's address. You open your book. If a person has moved three times, do you just pick out any address for that individual? No, you now look for the most recent address you have.

Although this is not a perfect analogy, there is a sense in which the Bible follows a similar pattern. Some of the ideas the inspired authors have written, like the address of those who have never moved, contain no further revelation. What you are reading reflects an idea that God has not developed or expanded on in Scripture. It is essentially presented with similar conclusions throughout the Bible.

Other ideas, however, have been added to and altered, as God continued to reveal more and more about himself and what he calls us to. By analogy, these would be compared to those people who have moved and changed their addresses.

Your address book now is a compilation of information taken at various stages of people's lives. Having said this though, would you describe those parts of your address book which are no longer current as inaccurate? You shouldn't. After all, they do accurately reflect the address and phone number of the person during the time it was marked in your book. They show a historical accuracy. In a similar way, the Bible is true and accurate. It reflects honestly the revelation of God for the period of time in which it was revealed. While some revelations were repeated without much change, other ideas were developed and expanded as other authors wrote.

It would not be fair to label parts of the Bible as "wrong" or "untruthful" or "misleading" any more that you would characterize your address book that way. Both books contain truth. The key is understanding how each is written. With the address book, it is a simple matter to look for the last address you have for someone, to know if it is current. With the Scriptures, as the books we have were not written in the order they were preserved, it is not as simple.

. Within a few days of September 11, 2001, shortly after the terrorist attack on the Twin Towers in New York, CNN aired an interview. They were asking various people what they felt the response of the United States should be. One person said that he wanted the "biblical idea of an eye for an eye and a tooth for a tooth." He was correct, that is a biblical quote. It is found in Deuteronomy 19:21 and Exodus 21:24. Even Jesus quotes it in Matthew 5:38, but then Christ goes on to give other commandments about how to deal with enemies. Jesus goes beyond the understanding of revenge found in some passages of the Bible. The man did find a correct scriptural quote, but he did not take into account later passages. Let's turn to some other examples:

> I am the LORD, there is no other;
> > I form the light, and create the darkness,
> I make well-being and create woe;
> > I, the LORD, do all these things.
>
> —Isaiah 45:6-7

There are some passages in the Old Testament that speak of God as the creator of difficulty and the cause of suffering. It would not be an authentic use of Scripture for everyone in pain to read such passages and automatically conclude that God is causing the difficulty they are going through. The revelations we have from Jesus depict more often a God who walks with us in our difficulty, rather than one who causes all our pain. In Scripture there is a development in the description of exactly how God deals with the world he has created. Jesus' description of the "Good Shepherd" is an example of that development. Compare the quote above from Isaiah with this one from the Gospel of John:

> I am the good shepherd. A good shepherd lays down his life for the sheep. A hired man, who is not a shepherd and whose sheep are not his own, sees a wolf coming and leaves the sheep and runs way, and the wolf catches and scatters them. This is because he works for pay and has no concern for the sheep. I am the good shepherd, and I know mine and mine know me, just as the Father knows me and I know the Father; and I will lay down my life for the sheep.
>
> —John 10:11-15

> All this I have kept in mind and recognized: the just, the wise, and their deeds are in the hand of God. Love from hatred man cannot tell; both appear equally vain, in that there is the same lot for all, for the just and the wicked, for the good and the bad, for the clean and the unclean, for him who offers sacrifice and him who does not. As it is for him who swears rashly, so it is for him who fears an oath. Among all things that happen under the sun, this is the worst, that things turn out the same for all.
>
> —Ecclesiastes 9:1-3

This passage reflects a common idea that was held before the revelation of Jesus, namely that when people die, regardless of how they lived their life, they would all end up the same. In some of the later books of the Old Testament, for example the book of Wisdom, and then certainly with the revelation of Jesus, a different idea is expressed:

> When the Son of Man comes in his glory, and all the angels with him, he will sit upon his glorious throne, and all the nations will be assembled before him. And he will separate them one from another, as the shepherd separates the sheep from the goats. He will place the sheep on his right and the goats on his left. Then the king will say to those on his right, "Come, you who are blessed by my Father. Inherit the kingdom prepared for you from the foundation of the world. For I was hungry and you gave me food, I was thirsty and you gave me drink, a stranger and you welcomed me, naked and you clothed me, ill and

you cared for me, in prison and you visited me." Then the righteous will answer him and say, "Lord, when did we see you hungry and feed you, or thirsty and give you drink? When did we see you a stranger and welcome you, or naked and clothe you? . . ." And the king will say to them in reply, "Amen, I say to you, whatever you did for one of these least brothers of mine, you did for me." Then he will say to those on his left, "Depart from me, you accursed, into the everlasting fire prepared for the devil and his angels. For I was hungry and you gave me no food, I was thirsty and you gave me no drink, a stranger and you gave me no welcome, naked and you gave me no clothing, ill and in prison, and you did not care for me." Then they will answer and say, "Lord, when did we see you hungry or thirsty or a stranger or naked or ill or in prison, and not minister to your needs?" He will answer them, "Amen, I say to you, what you did not do for one of these least ones, you did not do for me." And these will go off to eternal punishment, but the righteous to eternal life.

—Matthew 25:31-46

A passage such as this provides a more complete and fuller revelation than some of the earlier verses of the Bible that talk about the afterlife. Things don't necessarily turn out the same for everybody. At some point we are accountable for what we have done with our life.

Some time after these events, God put Abraham to the test. He called to him, "Abraham!" "Ready!" he replied. Then God said: "Take your son Isaac, your only one, whom you love, and go to the land of Moriah. There you shall offer him up as a holocaust on a height that I will point out to you. . . .

When they came to the place of which God had told him, Abraham built an altar there and tied up his son Isaac, and put him on top of the wood on the altar. Then he reached out and took the knife to slaughter his son. But the LORD's messenger called to him from heaven, "Abraham, Abraham!" "Yes, Lord," he answered. "Do not lay your hand on the boy," said the messenger. "Do not do the least thing to him. I know now how devoted you are to God, since you did not withhold from me your own beloved son."

—Genesis 22:1-2, 9-12

The meaning we often give to this passage is that it recalls the strength of Abraham's faith in God. However, some scholars suggest that originally the story centered around a different theme. During the time Abraham lived, human sacrifice was commonly practiced among Israel's neighbors, and sometimes even within Israel itself. Such events fostered the idea that there were occasions where the gods could be appeased only through human sacrifice. For example, 2 Kings 3:27 speaks of the King of Moab offering as a sacrifice his firstborn son. And so, this divine command might not have seemed too strange to Abraham. The original focus of the story, therefore, may have been to show that this God does not find human sacrifice acceptable. The account continues:

> As Abraham looked about, he spied a ram caught by its horns in the thicket. So he went and took the ram and offered it up as a holocaust in place of his son.
>
> —Genesis 22:13

This reference and many others in Scripture indicate the acceptance at some level, however, of the continuation of *animal* sacrifice. Even in New Testament times we know this practice was carried on:

> When the days were completed for their purification according to the law of Moses, they took him up to Jerusalem to present him to the Lord, just as it is written in the law of the Lord, "Every male that opens the womb shall be consecrated to the Lord," and to offer the sacrifice of "a pair of turtledoves or two young pigeons," in accordance with the dictate in the law of the Lord.
>
> —Luke 2:22-24

Then Jesus revisits the Old Testament (Isa 1:10-18; Ps 40:7-9, etc.) as he encourages the need for a different idea of sacrifice:

> "Which is the first of all the commandments?" Jesus replied, "The first is this: 'Hear, O Israel! The Lord our God is Lord alone! You shall love the Lord your God with all your heart, with all your soul, with all your mind, and with all your strength.' The second is this: 'You shall love your neighbor as yourself.' There is no other commandment greater than these." The scribe said to him, "Well said, teacher. You are right in saying, 'He is One and there is no other than he.' And 'to love him with all your heart, with all your understanding, with all your strength, and to love your neighbor as yourself' is worth more than all burnt offerings and sacrifices." And when Jesus saw that [he] answered with under-standing, he said to him, "You are not far from the kingdom of God."
>
> —Mark 12:28-34

In Scripture there is a development of this idea about sacrifice. From both animal and human sacrifice, to only animal sacrifice, to a new way of looking at what is most pleasing in God's eyes: the sacrifice that comes from within in loving God and neighbor.

Caution: In using this guideline, nowhere am I suggesting that the Old Testament is therefore irrelevant. While I have given some examples of how God has been revealed gradually over time, there are some significant Old Testament passages that even Jesus reiterates. The Old Testament contains God's Word revered by Jesus.

The novelty of the New Testament is not that it talks about love. "Take no revenge and cherish no grudge against your fellow countrymen. You shall love your neighbor as yourself." Sound familiar? The quote is from the Old Testament book of Leviticus 19:18. The Old Testament is neither defective nor outdated. It is the whole of Scripture that contains God's Word.

Nor am I suggesting that in the Old Testament we have a "God of fear" and in the New Testament we have a "God of love." There are certainly passages in the New Testament dealing with Jesus where he is stern and demanding, as well as sections in the Old Testament that describe God in very loving ways. It is in the Old Testament, for example, where God is described as a potter who shapes us; a shepherd who seeks us out; a gracious host who seats us at table and prepares a banquet; a mother bird who gathers us under her wings; and as a Father who picks us up when we fall.

This guideline is only suggesting that we be careful in our use of the Bible to realize that in some areas there is a later development of what is revealed in an earlier part of the Bible.

Some Words or Phrases Have a Special Meaning

Every so often during the year, the American Automobile Association makes certain predictions about how we travel. Last May the AAA predicted that 34 million Americans would travel during the Memorial Day weekend. They defined travel as "driving at least fifty miles from home." That isn't the only way to define the word "travel," but it was how they would use the word.

A store that sells cameras advertises that if you buy this item you will be given free film, "for the life of the camera." After this phrase there is an asterisk. The bottom of the advertisement defines "life of the camera" to be "two years from the date of purchase." That isn't the only way to define "life of the camera," but it is how the manufacturers chose to use it. If you purchase this camera you will get free film for two years, but no longer.

We can define how we want to use certain words. This is also seen when we read the Bible. Certain words and phrases have a particular meaning. Understanding the meaning of these words helps us when we interpret.

Amen, amen, I say to you, whoever believes has eternal life.

—John 6:47

Here Jesus is telling us that eternal life is connected to belief. We tend to look at belief as something that is just within the mind. But it would be an incorrect interpretation of this passage to suggest that all Jesus is asking of us is intellectual belief.

We believe that there is a place called China, although we have never been there. We believe the multiplication tables in math that we learned as a child to be true. Neither of these are exciting ideas, yet we believe them. For Jesus, his notion of belief is different. For him, it is to get so caught up in something and someone that it flows over into how we act and live our lives. "To believe" and "to do" are like the light and heat that come from a candle. They cannot be separated. One necessarily involves the other. This is a particular notion of what it means "to believe."

> Be on your guard! If your brother sins, rebuke him; and if he repents, forgive him. And if he wrongs you seven times in one day and returns to you seven times saying, "I am sorry," you should forgive him.
>
> —Luke 17:3-4

To give and to seek forgiveness are required of any Christian. It is one of the great paths to freedom. But just what does Jesus mean by the word "forgive"? It is something more than the popular "forgive and forget" that we sometimes hear. It would not be an authentic interpretation of this passage to suggest, for example, that as long as a spouse routinely comes home drunk and physically hurts his or her partner, but says "I'm sorry" each time, that the partner is obligated by God's command to forget the whole thing. To put together all the passages in the Bible where Jesus reveals what it means to forgive and to read those in the context of what he says about the value of the human individual, then we begin to get a clearer idea of what forgiveness means to him. Coming to learn what God tells us about how we relate to our neighbor involves looking at other ideas described by the biblical author. For example:

> Whatever town or village you enter, look for a worthy person in it, and stay there until you leave. As you enter a house, wish it peace. If the house is worthy, let your peace come upon it; if not, let your peace return to you. Whoever will not receive you or listen to your words—go outside that house or town and shake the dust from your feet. Amen, I say to you, it will be more tolerable for the land of Sodom and Gomorrah on the day of judgment than for that town.
>
> —Matthew 10:11-15

The disciples are told as they set out on their journey that when they are not listened to, they are to leave and have nothing to do with the town that would not receive them. That town will not be judged well by God.

There is also the admonition of Paul:

> We instruct you, brothers, in the name of [our] Lord Jesus Christ, to shun any brother who conducts himself in a disorderly way and not according to the tradition they have received from us.
>
> —2 Thessalonians 3:6

I am suggesting that the biblical ideas about how we are to relate to one another when things don't go as we would like deserve something more than just "forgive and forget." That phrase seems to imply that the Christian, when injured, should act as if nothing happened. But is that the standard God is asking us to follow? Both in Jesus' traveling instructions and in Paul's warning, certain steps are to be taken. Pretending things are fine does not seem to be one of them.

Doesn't it seem from the Bible that God is also looking for some degree of conversion in addition to the words "I'm sorry"? It is worthwhile to look at the Scriptures to find out what *God* means by the command "forgive," rather than assume God means only what many have come to expect.

> So Jesus said to them, "Amen, amen, I say to you, it was not Moses who gave the bread from heaven; my Father gives you the true bread from heaven. For the bread of God is that which comes down from heaven and gives life to the world."
>
> So they said to him, "Sir, give us this bread always." Jesus said to them, "I am the bread of life; whoever comes to me will never hunger, and whoever believes in me will never thirst."
>
> —John 6:32-35

Throughout the world thousands of people starve to death each day. Among them are followers of Jesus Christ. Some of them are people who gather to celebrate the Eucharist and receive Communion. But they die. How can that be, since Jesus tells us those who come to him will "neither hunger nor thirst"? It is because those words have a special meaning for Jesus. We can hunger and thirst for many things, not only food and water. Perhaps instead this is God's way of reminding us that in our spiritual life there is a special type of need that only God can fulfill.

In the English language we have what are called "figures of speech," phrases that have a meaning other than their literal meaning. For example, I've got an hour to kill, you're the apple of my eye, my feet are killing me, it's raining cats and dogs, this cup of coffee is "on the house."

None of these means exactly what it says. Many cultures share this same pattern in their verbal and written language. The same is true with certain passages of the Bible:

> Adam was one hundred and thirty years old when he begot a son in his likeness, after his image; and he named him Seth. Adam lived eight hundred years after the birth of Seth, and he had other sons and daughters. The whole lifetime of Adam was nine hundred and thirty years; then he died.
>
> When Seth was one hundred and five years old, he became the father of Enosh. Seth lived eight hundred and seven years after birth of Enosh, and he had other sons and daughters. The whole lifetime of Seth was nine hundred and twelve years; then he died.
>
> —Genesis 5:3-8

Sometimes in order to understand the Bible more, it helps to look at other things that were written at the same time as the books of the Bible. When we do this, we find that there was a figure of speech used at the time the book of Genesis was written that involved attributing "years" to a person's life. The more years that were mentioned could be either an indication of a greater influence that person had in his family or history, or a greater evaluation of the kind of life the person led. Such years were not meant to be taken literally, but were a figure of speech well understood by the people of the time. As the authors of the Bible would have been influenced as any author by the style of writing of the day, it is easy to see how they would have used these figures of speech from time to time in their own writing. One of the keys in interpreting Scripture is to expand our understanding of how truth is conveyed, rather than limiting it to a twenty-first-century understanding of historical accuracy. Sometimes what a verse says is not the truth it means.

> On the third day there was a wedding in Cana in Galilee, and the mother of Jesus was there. Jesus and his disciples were also invited to the wedding. When the wine ran short, the mother of Jesus said to him, "They have no wine." [And] Jesus said to her, "Woman, how does your concern affect me? My hour has not yet come." His mother

said to the servers, "Do whatever he tells you." Now there were six
stone water jars there for Jewish ceremonial washings . . . .

—John 2:1-6

This familiar story has an interesting detail. The number of water jars
is six. The number six was used to show that something was incomplete
or unfinished. It has a special symbolic meaning. This is seen in other
passages. Recall there are six days of creation. Something about creation
is not complete until God makes a day holy. The scriptural number asso-
ciated with the devil is 666. The number three signifies perfection. To
have three sixes might be a way of saying the devil is "perfectly" or "the
most" incomplete of all beings.

At the wedding feast, perhaps the six jars are a reminder that there is
something unfinished about us until we are transformed, as the wine
was. The number six, as well as some other numbers in the Bible, has a
special meaning.

"I am the Alpha and the Omega," says the Lord God, "the one who is
and who was and who is to come, the almighty."

—Revelation 1:8

"Alpha" is the first letter of the Greek alphabet. "Omega" is the last
letter. The book of Revelation uses this figure to identify God as the beginning and end of all. Just as those two letters form the framework of
an alphabet, all reality can be seen as connected to God. The author reiterates the meaning of this phrase when he concludes that God is almighty.
This phrase and several others in the book of Revelation have a special
meaning. That is one of the reasons this particular book of the Bible is
challenging to interpret.

There Can Be a Difference between Personal Experience and Divine Teaching

Masters, treat your slaves justly and fairly, realizing that you too have
a Master in heaven.

—Colossians 4:1

Slavery was a part of the lifestyle of some of Saint Paul's readers. That
personal experience described at the time of slavery is not the same
thing as God's justification of the practice. Too many passages in Scrip-

ture speak of the dignity and freedom of the individual to have us believe that God condones owning another human being. This passage reflects the personal experience of the time, but is not Divine teaching recommending the continuation of slavery.

> Why do you reject me, LORD?
>   Why hide your face from me?
> I am mortally afflicted since youth;
>   lifeless, I suffer your terrible blows.
> Your wrath has swept over me;
>   your terrors have reduced me to silence.
> All the day they surge round like a flood;
>   from every side they close in on me.
> Because of you companions shun me;
>   my only friend is darkness.
>
> —Psalm 88:15-19

These are strong words that convey a lot of emotion. The author of this psalm is describing an intense experience of feeling abandoned by God. While it is how he feels at the time, it would not be fair to automatically presume that God has in fact abandoned him, and that it is God who has ruined his life. Throughout the pages of Scripture we read about different people's experiences with God. As in our own life, however, we need to make room for the possibility that a difficult personal experience we go through might not be caused by God.

> Now this is how the birth of Jesus Christ came about. When his mother Mary was betrothed to Joseph, but before they lived together, she was found with child through the holy Spirit. Joseph her husband, since he was a righteous man, yet unwilling to expose her to shame, decided to divorce her quietly. Such was his intention when, behold, the angel of the Lord appeared to him in a dream and said, "Joseph, son of David, do not be afraid to take Mary your wife into your home. For it is through the holy Spirit that this child has been conceived in her. She will bear a son and you are to name him Jesus, because he will save his people from their sins."
>
> —Matthew 1:18-21

Over the years, techniques involving artificial ways to reproduce a new life have become more commonplace. Some people have used passages like this one saying that it shows God approves of using surrogate parents or other procedures where new life is created through some means other than intercourse between husband and wife. However, the personal experience of Mary and Joseph described here is not the same as an endorsement of medical techniques which would be developed centuries later.

> They devoted themselves to the teaching of the apostles and to the communal life, to the breaking of the bread and to the prayers. Awe came upon everyone, and many wonders and signs were done through the apostles. All who believed were together and had all things in common; they would sell their property and possessions and divide them among all according to each one's need.
>
> —Acts 2:42-45

After Jesus died it was believed by many of the early Christians that the end of the world was approaching. It was this belief that would have influenced how they acted, and helps explain certain aspects of their "communal" life such as selling all they had. This personal experience of theirs would not make it mandatory for us to do the same.

> In the course of that night, however, Jacob arose, took his two wives, with the two maidservants and his eleven children, and crossed the ford of the Jabbok.
>
> —Genesis 32:23

Although there is a reference to Jacob having two wives at the same time, this could hardly be interpreted as God revealing that either bigamy or unfaithfulness to one's wife is acceptable. As ideas about commitment are recorded in the New Testament writings, there is a development in the notion of fidelity and the marriage covenant.

In the Bible, sometimes personal experience needs to be distinguished from divine teaching.

Sometimes Exaggeration Is Used to Make a Point

The writings of different cultures have some similarities between them. One of these is the ability to exaggerate in order to make a point. As long as it's seen for what it is, to exaggerate is not to deceive. More often than not exaggerating is done in a way in which it is clear to the listener that the speaker is exaggerating. This can occur, for example, because a common phrase is used where people know it is not meant to be taken literally. It shouldn't be surprising that this type of writing has found its way into the Bible. While it does not seem to occur often, there are times where it is used in order to make a point or draw someone's attention to the importance of what is being said:

> If your hand causes you to sin, cut it off. It is better for you to enter into life maimed than with two hands to go into Gehenna, into the unquenchable fire. And if your foot causes you to sin, cut it off. It is better for you to enter into life crippled than with two feet to be thrown into Gehenna. And if your eye causes you to sin, pluck it out. Better for you to enter into the kingdom of God with one eye than with two eyes to be thrown into Gehenna, where "their worm does not die, and the fire is not quenched."
>
> —Mark 9:43-48

It doesn't at all seem consistent with what God teaches about the sanctity of life that he expects us to literally carry this out. This would be an example where it would seem God means something other than the literal words of what he says. This may be an exaggerated idea to help us focus on the evil of sin. A person can work at being obedient to God in ways that don't involve self-mutilation.

> Amen, amen, I say to you, I am the gate for the sheep. All who came [before me] are thieves and robbers, but the sheep did not listen to them.
>
> —John 10:7-8

For Jesus to characterize *all* who came before him as "thieves and robbers" seems to be something of an exaggeration in order to make a point. Elsewhere in the Bible Jesus is generous with his praise of some who have gone before him. He would admit "among those born of women there has been none greater than John the Baptist" (Matt 11:11). And in talking to Solomon God says, "there has never been anyone like you up to now, and after you there will come no one to equal you" (1 Kgs 3:12). Those are hardly the attributes of thieves or robbers. In this passage from John, by exaggerating Jesus may be helping us see that compared to all who came before him, he is the one true shepherd we are to follow, the only "gate for the sheep."

Amen, I say to you, whoever says to this mountain, "Be lifted up and thrown into the sea," and does not doubt in his heart but believes that what he says will happen, it shall be done for him.

—Mark 11:23

As the disciples are walking along, Saint Mark tells us they see a withered fig tree that Jesus had cursed. While walking outside, Jesus points to a mountain and makes his claim. However, no matter how much you believe, your belief is not going to cause a mountain to move. This exaggerated statement is calling for us to put faith in God, even for things that might seem difficult in our life, but it is not meant to be taken literally.

Great crowds were traveling with him, and he turned and addressed them, "If anyone comes to me without hating his father and mother, wife and children, brothers and sisters, and even his own life, he cannot be my disciple."

—Luke 14:25-26

Every year the Catholic Church initiates adults into its community of faith. Members of a parish typically help those involved to discern their call. I couldn't imagine giving someone the impression that as part of a way to discern God's call the individual should reflect on whether or not hatred for family is at a high enough level to match the standard Jesus sets in this passage for discipleship.

To take this directive of Jesus literally would be to contradict so many other passages of the Bible, such as, "Honor your father and your mother" (Mark 10:19), and, "Children, obey your parents in everything, for this is pleasing to the Lord" (Col 3:20).

Maybe Jesus is exaggerating to make a valuable point. He may be suggesting the importance of making sure that family members do not get in the way of our response to God. Family members can do this by their example, such as a parent not practicing his or her faith; discussions at the dinner table that put down God or Church; remarks by adults that lead young people in the family to conclude that faith doesn't mean much.

These can all be ways that family members can hurt the growth of faith. The kind of dedication Jesus asks for is one in which we do not allow people or things to hinder God's ability to reach us and our desire to be with God.

Caution: While this guideline is applicable to a few passages, it doesn't seem that it applies to too many. We have to be careful not to put a verse in this category just because it might be difficult to follow. For example, to say the commands "love your enemies" or "forgive one another" are exaggerations would not be using this principle correctly. It seems more likely that a word or phrase is exaggerated when, if taken literally, it goes against some other teaching of Jesus.

Some Knowledge of Tradition Is Helpful

I have much more to tell you, but you cannot bear it now.

—John 16:12

Now Jesus did many other signs in the presence of [his] disciples that are not written in this book.

—John 20:30

Go, therefore, and make disciples of all nations, baptizing them in the name of the Father, and of the Son, and of the holy Spirit, teaching them to observe all that I have commanded you. And behold, I am with you always, until the end of the age.

—Matthew 28:19-20

There are also many other things that Jesus did, but if these were to be described individually, I do not think the whole world would contain the books that would be written.

—John 21:25

These passages speak of God's continued revelation, which takes place not only in how we interpret Scripture, but also in how God continues to influence and guide the day to day mission of the Church.

It is worth recognizing that there are any number of theological terms that are used in religious discussion that are not found in the Bible. Words such as sacrament, Trinity, purgatory, confirmation, and annulment are not found in the pages of the Bible, and yet these and other words reflect notions that are used in the Catholic experience. Some understanding of the tradition of our faith and how it relates to Scripture is helpful in interpreting the Bible in an authentic manner.

One of the most important ideas in Catholic biblical interpretation is the understanding that the Bible must be read within the context of tradition and the life of the Church. Remember, both the Church and tradition preceded the coming into being of the Bible. Therefore, they provide the context for the correct interpretation of Scripture. The Church, tradition, and Scripture are so intertwined that one cannot stand without the others.

We have never had the sense that with the Bible being written, God has stopped guiding and inspiring. Tradition reflects this ongoing presence of God. A church without tradition would be a church with amnesia, forever starting over without a memory of the past. Revelation involves dialogue. It is, in part, brought about as we respond to God's continuous call. Believing that God is always with us, we hold fast to the influence of the Holy Spirit continuing to direct us.

> But from the beginning of creation, "God made them male and female. For this reason a man shall leave his father and mother [and be joined to his wife], and the two shall become one flesh." So they are no longer two but one flesh. Therefore what God has joined together, no human being must separate.
>
> —Mark 10:6-9

What is it that Jesus says no human being must separate? It is "what God has joined together." Are all people who enter into marriage automatically "joined by God"? At first this seems like a simple enough question. But what about countries that allow a man to be married to more than one wife at a time? Does God recognize all marriages that are legal, even though what makes a marriage legal differs throughout the world? Are those who enter into same sex unions recognized by a state "joined by God"? How do Jesus' ideas about divorce apply? These are important questions to answer, as it is the marriages "joined by God" that cannot be ended. But the Scriptures alone do not provide a simple answer. Over the centuries, ideas that have developed about divorce, annulment, and sacrament help us in a sense to "fill in" some of what Scripture is less clear about. These ideas are not simply random conclusions, but rather form part of our tradition, which we feel has been guided by the Spirit.

> When the sabbath came he began to teach in the synagogue, and many who heard him were astonished. They said, "Where did this man get all this? What kind of wisdom has been given him? What mighty deeds are wrought by his hands! Is he not the carpenter, the son of Mary, and the brother of James and Joses and Judas and Simon? And are not his sisters here with us?"
>
> —Mark 6:2-3

This passage speaks of the brothers and sisters of Jesus. This phrase is used in other places of the New Testament as well. How can it be interpreted? Over the centuries different notions have been brought forward to help demonstrate that this is not a reference to "blood" brothers or sisters. For example, when Jesus is on the cross, he puts Mary under the care of John. If there were blood relatives in the family other than Jesus, why wouldn't Mary have been entrusted to one or more of them? There are also other passages in Scripture where the phrase "brothers and sisters" matches more our understanding of "cousin" or "relative." We can add to this the observation that nowhere in the Bible does it say that these brothers and sisters of Jesus are actually the children of Mary. One theory suggests that Joseph was married once before. He was a widower at the time he married Mary. These are Joseph's children from his first marriage that Mary raised as her own. However, with all of these ideas it is difficult to use only the evidence found within the Bible to prove the exact meaning of the phrase "brothers and sisters of Jesus."

It is within the Catholic tradition, as well as that of some Protestant faiths, that Mary remained a virgin. This conclusion comes from Christian reflection on the sanctity of her life. For us, it is this belief that clarifies whatever uncertainty the Scriptures themselves do not resolve.

> Then God delivered all these commandments:
> "I, the LORD, am your God, who brought you out of the land of Egypt, that place of slavery. You shall not have other gods besides me. . . . Remember to keep holy the sabbath day."
>
> —Exodus 20:1-3, 8

While the Bible itself does not equate the "third commandment" with celebrating the Eucharist each weekend, our tradition has developed in a way that connects the obligation to participate at Mass with keeping holy the sabbath.

In part, our development of tradition has something to do with authority and how it is exercised in the Church, as seen in the next passage:

> I will give you the keys to the kingdom of heaven. Whatever you bind on earth shall be bound in heaven; and whatever you loose on earth shall be loosed in heaven.
>
> —Matthew 16:19

God has given the Church authority to act and make decisions; however, these words of Jesus to Saint Peter remind us of how important it is to be open to the guidance of God and the work of the Spirit, for that is where true authority comes from.

Every Word Counts

Recently I received a notice in the mail from the place I bought my car. It described what they referred to as a "special one day offer." I was told that if I brought my car back to the dealer they would give me "up to $17,000 toward the purchase" of my next car. This seemed like an offer I couldn't pass up. But when I took my car in, I was told that I would be getting $4000. It was my mistake. I saw the "$17,000," but didn't notice the two words in small print that came before it: "up to." I wasn't going to be offered $17,000, but *up to* that amount. It was a reminder to me that skipping over a word or two can make a difference in what something means. This is true of Scripture as well. You don't want to skip over any words or phrases.

Once we have heard stories from the Bible often enough, there may be a tendency not to listen as closely. In addition to the challenge this presents, many people bring some preconceived ideas to the Scriptures, which sometimes are not very accurate.

For example, while we might think there were three Magi who brought gifts to the child Jesus, the Bible does not reveal their number. Some might believe that Eve ate an apple from the tree, but the book of Genesis doesn't even have the word "apple" in it. In art we have seen Saint Paul fall off his horse at the time of his conversion. While the Bible does tell us he "fell to the ground" it does not say he was riding anything. We remember that on that first Pentecost there were "tongues of fire" that rested above those gathered in the room. Yet the Bible actually says "tongues *as of* fire." Whatever it was, it was something different than anything they had seen before. It may have resembled fire, but the Bible doesn't say that it was.

While the observations above are not major, they do remind us that one of the challenges in hearing the Scriptures proclaimed or reading them ourselves is to hear or see what is actually there. As we read God's Word it can be easy to focus on those verses that simply reinforce conclusions to which we have already come. The danger with Scripture is similar to the danger we face with one another: that we will see only what we want to see. Paying careful attention to each of the inspired words of the Bible helps us to avoid that. For the careful reader, God's revealed Word still holds surprises:

But as it is written:
    "What eye has not seen, and ear has not heard,

and what has not entered the human heart,
what God has prepared for those who love him."

—1 Corinthians 2:9

The last phrase "for those who love him" is an important part of this quote. Without it, it could be possible to interpret the passage as an indication that there is no such thing as being accountable for what we have done with our life.

Then he told them a parable. "There was a rich man whose land produced a bountiful harvest. He asked himself, 'What shall I do, for I do not have space to store my harvest?' And he said, 'This is what I shall do: I shall tear down my barns and build larger ones. There I shall store all my grain and other goods and I shall say to myself, "Now as for you, you have so many good things stored up for many years, rest, eat, drink, be merry!"' But God said to him, 'You fool, this night your life will be demanded of you; and the things you have prepared, to whom will they belong?' Thus will it be for the one who stores up treasure for himself but is not rich in what matters to God."

—Luke 12:16-21

An important part of Jesus' teaching is contained in the last few words of the parable. Had Jesus only said, "thus will it be for the one who stores up treasure for himself," then the meaning of the parable would be limited more to the idea that wealth and possessions get in the way of our developing a connection to God. But in order to understand more completely what Jesus is teaching, we don't want to think that Christ's admonition ends there. His sentence continues with another phrase. The entire last sentence reads: "Thus will it be for the one who stores up treasure for himself but is not rich in what matters to God." The ultimate concern of Jesus is not whether someone has possessions, but whether that person has "grown rich" with God. To be sure, wealthy people have the same ability to develop spiritually as anyone else.

Everyone's state in life carries its own particular challenges in being close to God. If you are wealthy there is one set of challenges; if you are poor there is another set. Here, Jesus is less concerned that the man in the parable is rich than the fact that he got that way instead of growing rich with God.

Jesus then went down to Capernaum, a town of Galilee. He taught them on the sabbath, and they were astonished at his teaching because he spoke with authority. In the synagogue there was a man with the spirit of an unclean demon, and he cried out in a loud voice, "Ha! What have you to do with us, Jesus of Nazareth? Have you come to destroy us? I know who you are—the Holy One of God!" Jesus rebuked him and said, "Be quiet! Come out of him!" Then the demon threw the man down in front of them and came out of him without doing him any harm.

—Luke 4:31-36

In this story, who is it that recognizes that Christ is the Holy One of God? While Jesus' intervention is witnessed by those in the synagogue, the one who proclaims the truth is the demon. As every word is important, it is worth noting that here it is the "outsider" who sees something that others do not. This happens elsewhere in Scripture. In Mark's Gospel, for example, as Jesus is being crucified, it is the pagan Roman guard who proclaims him to be God's Son (Mark 15:39). Passages such as these should keep us humble. Sometimes those whom we think are the least connected to God can see things that we are unable to see.

Filled with the holy Spirit, Jesus returned from the Jordan and was led by the Spirit into the desert for forty days, to be tempted by the devil. He ate nothing during those days, and when they were over he was hungry.

—Luke 4:1-3

The desert did not provide a life of ease. A lack of food, water, and safety were all concerns. One word can be singled out in these verses to provide some added meaning to this passage. It is the Spirit that leads Jesus into the desert. Reflecting on this allows us to recognize that sometimes this same Spirit can lead us into "desert experiences" as well. There are times in our lives when the Spirit leads us into and through some difficulty. Perhaps this is done to help us see more clearly that we are not as self-sufficient as we might think. This is not to say that God is the cause of all the challenges we face, only that there can be occasions where God makes use of them.

Not All Stories Are Meant to Be Imitated Exactly as They Are Described

Sometimes in Jesus' parables and teachings, instead of giving us laws he is offering examples. In other words, not everything recorded in the

Bible is meant to be followed as if it were a literal command. Some of Jesus' stories challenge us to see what he says as an example which has to be translated into each generation and culture:

> But I say to you, offer no resistance to one who is evil. When someone strikes you on [your] right cheek, turn the other one to him as well. If anyone wants to go to law with you over your tunic, hand him your cloak as well. Should anyone press you into service for one mile, go with him for two miles.
>
> —Matthew 5:39-41

If these words are interpreted as literal laws or commands, they would suggest that God is telling us not to remove ourselves from situations where we are being hit; to freely hand over to someone what is asked for, even if it is an unjust request; and not to seek an opportunity to escape from someone who kidnaps us. If these are laws, they do not seem to correspond to the other teachings of Jesus. However, if we see them as examples, then they take on a whole other meaning.

Turning your cheek might very well be an example of Jesus stressing that you should not allow your honor or dignity to come between you and another. Handing over your coat as well as your tunic might suggest that relationships are more important than property. Staying with someone for two miles suggests that your time is not more important than people.

Taken as laws the remarks of Jesus don't make much sense, but as examples they are reminders of how to keep certain priorities before us.

> He sat down opposite the treasury and observed how the crowd put money into the treasury. Many rich people put in large sums. A poor widow also came and put in two small coins worth a few cents. Calling his disciples to himself, he said to them, "Amen, I say to you, this poor widow put in more than all the other contributors to the treasury. For they have all contributed from their surplus wealth, but she, from her poverty, has contributed all she had, her whole livelihood."
>
> —Mark 12:41-44

It would not be an authentic interpretation of this passage to suggest that Jesus is calling each of us to give away all we have, "our whole livelihood," in imitation of the widow. All that would accomplish would be to transfer poverty from one to another. It would do nothing to deal with the issue of poverty, as it would remain at the same level as before.

Jesus is not offering us a literal law to follow. In fact, in this passage he does not even ask us to do what the widow did. However, if seen as an example then the story has more meaning. It can be seen as a challenge to be generous, but perhaps there is even a deeper example being provided. This widow had no spouse and now, having given her livelihood away, no money. Having given away "all she had," perhaps all that was left in her life now was God. Maybe Jesus is offering an example of encouraging us not to wait until the end of our life until we get ourselves into the situation she did—where we begin to seriously face God.

The kingdom of heaven is like a landowner who went out at dawn to hire laborers for his vineyard. After agreeing with them for the usual daily wage, he sent them into his vineyard. Going out about nine o'clock, he saw others standing idle in the marketplace, and he said to them, "You too go into my vineyard, and I will give you what is just." So they went off. [And] he went out again around noon, and around three o'clock, and did likewise. Going out about five o'clock, he found others standing around, and said to them, "Why do you stand here idle all day?" They answered, "Because no one has hired us." He said to them, "You too go into my vineyard." When it was evening the owner of the vineyard said to his foreman, "Summon the laborers and give them their pay, beginning with the last and ending with the first." When those who had started about five o'clock came, each received the usual daily wage. So when the first came, they thought that they would receive more, but each of them also got the usual wage. And on receiving it, they grumbled against the landowner, saying, "These last ones worked only one hour, and you have made them equal to us, who bore the day's burden and the heat." He said to one of them in reply, "My friend, I am not cheating you. Did you not agree with me for the usual daily wage? Take what is yours and go. What if I wish to give this last one the same as you? [Or] am I not free to do as I wish with my own money? Are you envious because I am generous?" Thus the last will be first, and the first will be last.

—Matthew 20:1-16

If taken as a law, no one who is an employer would remain in business long. However, if Jesus offers an example, then there is more meaning to his words. Perhaps an interpretation of the passage indicates the idea that the value of our life is not dependent on the results we produce. The person in the wheelchair is not less valuable in God's eyes, because he or she cannot produce as much as someone else. The same is true of the unborn who may not yet be seen as "productive members of society."

The person in the coma still deserves to be treated with respect. Our value in life shouldn't be determined by what we can accomplish at any given time.

Then God delivered all these commandments:

"I, the LORD, am your God, who brought you out of the land of Egypt, that place of slavery. You shall not have other gods besides me. . . .

"You shall not take the name of the LORD, your God, in vain. . . .

"Remember to keep holy the sabbath day. . . .

"Honor your father and your mother. . . .

"You shall not kill.

"You shall not commit adultery.

"You shall not steal.

"You shall not bear false witness against your neighbor.

"You shall not covet your neighbor's house. You shall not covet your neighbor's wife."

—Exodus 20:1-3, 7-8, 12-17

Most of us would recognize that it is possible to literally keep each of these commandments, and yet still be seriously lacking in how we follow God. If we choose to view the commandments only as literal laws to follow, we can obey them, but still find ourselves not connected to their author. But if in addition to being laws they also provide for us examples of the values that God is calling us to live, then their meaning grows and we have a better appreciation for what God calls us to. We are not just asked to obey ten rules, but to also respect their underlying values: worship of God, truth, human life, sexuality, and justice.

So to them he addressed this parable. "What man among you having a hundred sheep and losing one of them would not leave the ninety-nine in the desert and go after the lost one until he finds it? And when he does find it, he sets it on his shoulders with great joy and, upon his arrival home, he calls together his friends and neighbors and says to them, 'Rejoice with me because I have found my lost sheep.' I tell you, in just the same way there will be more joy in heaven over one sinner who repents than over ninety-nine righteous people who have no need of repentance."

—Luke 15:3-7

This parable was not meant to be imitated by the shepherds exactly as Jesus described it. He was not offering advice on how they should do their work. For while a shepherd could relate to happiness in finding a lost sheep, not many of them would find it an acceptable practice to leave ninety-nine sheep alone in the desert. Without food, water, or protection the ninety-nine might not even be there by the time the shepherd returned from his journey of finding the one that was lost.

Instead, this parable has lessons to it that are similar to the story of the prodigal son, which Luke includes in this same chapter of his Gospel. It is a reminder to us that God looks for what has left him.

Do we make efforts to do the same? Are there things in our lives that we have lost? Do we make an effort to find them? What "sheep" have gotten away from us?

One person may have lost the ability to forgive. Such a person stores up hurt in his or her memory. Maybe forgiveness was easy in the person's youth, but since then it has gone away.

Another may have lost the ability to believe. Death or unemployment or disease may have filled such a person with the idea that God, even if God is alive, has long since left.

This parable can serve as a reminder to us that even though something has been lost it can sometimes still be found again. Not only does God show an interest in searching, but sometimes so should we.

Chapter 4

Discover

One of the goals in reading the Bible is to arrive at an interpretation that is consistent with a message that God would like us to hear. The guidelines that were explained in the previous chapter described ways that can be used to help us stay within the boundaries of interpreting the Scriptures with this in mind.

When it comes to interpreting God's Word, there are different "levels" of meaning that can be found. This is true not only of Scripture, but also of relationships with others. We do not relate to everyone we know on the same level.

I would suggest that there are three levels of how we relate to others. These apply not only to human relationships, but also to how we relate to the living words of the Bible.

The first level is that of *recognition*. Have you ever had the experience of walking into a room of people and recognizing someone? You might not know anything else about the face you see, but you do recognize the person . . . from somewhere. This is not a very significant level of awareness. Some people relate to the Bible only in this way. For example, Arlene goes to church on Sunday morning. At the time for the gospel reading to be proclaimed she hears these words: "Jesus said to the crowd: 'You are the salt of the earth.'" She immediately recognizes the statement since she has heard it before. She even knows from memory what the next sentence is. But she has no further insight into the passage. She does not know what it means to be likened to salt, and is unsure of its significance. She recognizes the passage, but for whatever reason does not go further.

The second level involves *being aware of the obvious*. Paul is talking to a friend. In the course of their conversation Paul asks his friend if he knows Leanne. His friend isn't sure, and asks Paul who she is. Paul does not know her well, but replies by giving a description. He mentions her height, hair color, and the fact that she wears glasses . . . things that would be obvious to someone who had seen her. He also knows a few facts: she is married and lives in the same city he does. Beyond that he admits to knowing little about her. This is more than the recognition described in the previous paragraph. Here, certain things are known, but the person remains something of a mystery.

Sometimes our understanding of a passage reaches this second level of awareness. We can hear or read something from Scripture. We not only recognize the passage, but have some sense of what it means. Our understanding of the passage though does not go beyond what is obvious. For example, on Easter Sunday a parishioner hears the story of Jesus rising from the dead. Before the homily is ever given, this listener knows that Jesus' Resurrection is a reminder that there is life after death for us all. There is not only recognition of the passage, but some sense of its most obvious meaning.

The third level of awareness begins to *look beneath the surface,* to recognize what the casual observer is unaware of. If someone is a friend and you know that person well enough, you are probably at this level of awareness. You would recognize the person in a room. You could state the obvious by giving a physical description and recalling a few facts about the person's life. But there is also something deeper. You know how the person feels about a given topic or a goal he or she has in life. You might even be able to anticipate what that person will say in a conversation. These are all facets of the individual that are beneath the surface. We can relate to Scripture in this way as well. Through praying, listening, and reading we can become ever more aware of the great variety of ways that God speaks to us through the Word.

As we interpret the Bible, we do try to discern the meaning of the original author's words. However, we are not limited to that alone. We can also take a passage and find some added meaning. For example, driving on a long stretch of highway you come upon a billboard that reads "Running on empty?" Seeing the sign, you instinctively look to the gauge of your gas tank to be sure you have enough gas. However, if you look back at the sign you see that next to the question is an arrow pointing to a McDonald's restaurant. The author of the billboard meant for you to think about your stomach being on "empty," not your gas tank. But you are not limited to interpreting the billboard exclusively with the single intended message. Whether it involves getting something to eat—which means you must stop driving and take a break—or making sure you can make it to the next exit, in either case the general idea of safety is promoted. If the billboard has helped you not run out of gas, then it has served an additional worthwhile purpose.

Another analogy may help. "Word association" is a process where a spoken word is meant to trigger a response. An interviewer says a word and the listener is supposed to say the first word that comes to mind. In response to "on" you might say "off." You hear "color" and reply "blue." To the word "up" perhaps your response is "down." It is the first thought that comes to your mind when you hear the word. We can apply this to God's Word as well. We hear a particular parable or a saying of Jesus, and an idea comes to mind. But unlike "word association" we can (and should) look further. Just as the hearer of the word "up" could say a series of words (sky, heaven, stars, etc.), so too we can look beyond the first thought we have when God speaks to us.

God's Word speaks to people of every generation. As we read and interpret it, we work at opening its meaning in as many ways as are consistent with authentic communication from God. There are several different ways that can help us in this process of looking beneath the surface of the passages in Scripture. Before we go further, we can consider five of them.

Look for Patterns and Then See How the Pattern Changes

> Then God said, "Let there be light" . . . .
> Then God said, "Let there be a dome in the middle of the waters . . . ."
> Then God said, "Let the water under the sky be gathered . . . ."
> Then God said, "Let the earth bring forth vegetation . . . ."
> Then God said: "Let there be lights in the dome of the sky . . . ."
> Then God said, "Let the water teem with an abundance of living creatures . . . ."
> Then God said, "Let the earth bring forth all kinds of living creatures . . . ." Then God said: "Let us make man in our image, after our likeness. Let them have dominion over the fish of the sea, the birds of the air, and the cattle, and over all the wild animals and all the creatures that crawl on the ground."
>
> —Genesis 1:3, 6, 9, 11, 14, 20, 24, 26

The first chapter of Genesis contains some definite patterns. God says what God wants to create, and it is created. Evening comes and morning follows, and the next thing is created. This is the basic pattern found in the days of creation. But then, some of the pattern changes when God creates people. It is only right before the first human is created that the Bible describes God as almost thinking about what God intends to do. While God certainly gave thought to all of that was created, in Genesis it is most evident prior to the creation of human beings. And then after that act of creation there is another change in the pattern. God blesses the newest creation and goes on to describe what God wants for us. This change in the pattern of what goes into our creation helps signify the importance of human life, the value inherent in each of us, and the responsibility we have to be caretakers of the earth. We are different from anything else God created!

Peter began to say to him, "We have given up everything and followed you." Jesus said, "Amen, I say to you, there is no one who has given up house or brothers or sisters or mother or father or children or lands for my sake and for the sake of the gospel who will not receive a hundred times now in this present age: houses and brothers and sisters and mothers and children and lands, with persecutions, and eternal life in the age to come."

—Mark 10:28-30

These verses contain two lists: what is given up and what is received. Everything in the first list is included in the second, with one exception. Look at the words in both lists again. Do you see the difference? Jesus' followers are promised a hundred times everything they have given up, except in the second list the mention of "father" is not included. It reflects a change of the pattern. This may be Jesus' way of stressing that ultimately we all have only one Father, who is in heaven (Matt 23:9 and 1 Cor 4:15). He is sufficient, and so we do not get a hundred times as many fathers.

Filled with the holy Spirit, Jesus returned from the Jordan and was led by the Spirit into the desert for forty days, to be tempted by the devil. He ate nothing during those days, and when they were over he was hungry. The devil said to him, "If you are the Son of God, command this stone to become bread." Jesus answered him, "It is written, 'One does not live by bread alone.'" Then he took him up and showed him all the kingdoms of the world in a single instant. The devil said to him, "I shall give to you all this power and their glory; for it has been handed over to me, and I may give it to whomever I wish. All this will be yours if you worship me." Jesus said to him in reply, "It is written:
   'You shall worship the Lord, your God,
     and him alone shall you serve.'"

Then he led him to Jerusalem, made him stand on the parapet of the temple, and said to him, "If you are the Son of God, throw yourself down from here, for it is written:
'He will command his angels concerning you,
to guard you,'
and:
'With their hands they will support you,
lest you dash your foot against a stone.'"

—Luke 4:1-11

There is a pattern in this story of the three temptations. Part of the pattern is the use of Scripture. In response to each temptation, a quote from Scripture is made. After the first temptation, Jesus is the one who quotes the Bible. After the second temptation, Jesus again quotes the Bible. However, the pattern changes after the third temptation, when it is the devil who quotes from Scripture.

One interpretation of this passage can focus on where the pattern changes: the devil's use of something holy—the Bible. This may be a reminder to us that even good things, for example religion, can be used to tempt us, because in religion we can do things that have the appearance of being holy, without ever changing to become better. We can, as the devil did, use holy things to actually avoid an honest journey to God.

I myself will pasture my sheep; I myself will give them rest, says the Lord GOD. The lost I will seek out, the strayed I will bring back, the injured I will bind up, the sick I will heal [but the sleek and the strong I will destroy], shepherding them rightly.

—Ezekiel 34:15-16

There is a pattern to how this verse begins. God is telling us of his compassion: the lost God will seek out; the strayed God will bring back; the injured and the sick God will help. In these phrases there is a challenge (lost, strayed, or injured) and then a positive remedy is provided (seek out, bring back, help). But then the pattern changes, and God announces "the sleek and the strong I will destroy." What happened to the compassion God was showing? Where is the remedy? There are any number of things you could say in interpreting this passage, but we can also focus on the change of this pattern. Perhaps it is a reminder that certain kinds of strength can be detrimental to our spirituality. For example, a person can be so strong as to always be helping others but never allowing others (including God) to help them. Perhaps God is not anxious to encourage strength such as this. Some of this idea is carried through when Saint Paul writes:

> Rather, God chose the foolish of the world to shame the wise, and God chose the weak of the world to shame the strong, and God chose the lowly and despised of the world, those who count for nothing, to reduce to nothing those who are something, so that no human being might boast before God.
>
> —1 Corinthians 1:27-29

> On leaving the synagogue he entered the house of Simon and Andrew with James and John. Simon's mother-in-law lay sick with a fever. They immediately told him about her. He approached, grasped her hand, and helped her up. Then the fever left her and she waited on them.
>
> —Mark 1:29-31

There are certain elements common among healing stories in the New Testament. One of those elements is not found here. Usually when Jesus heals he does so using words. This is one of those few times where healing occurs with Jesus saying nothing. That change in a pattern may not seem significant, but perhaps it can remind us of the benefit of simply being present to people who are in need, even if we don't have all the right words to help make them feel better. Just being in the same room with someone who suffers, even if no words are exchanged, can make a difference.

> When John heard in prison of the works of the Messiah, he sent his disciples to him with this question, "Are you the one who is to come, or should we look for another?" Jesus said to them in reply, "Go and tell John what you hear and see: the blind regain their sight, the lame walk, lepers are cleansed, the deaf here, the dead are raised, and the poor have the good news proclaimed to them."
>
> —Matthew 11:2-5

The words that Jesus tells to John's disciples contain a pattern. There is an affliction and then the opposite occurs: the blind regain their sight, the lame walk, lepers are cleansed, the deaf hear, the dead are raised. If the pattern were to continue, Jesus would then have said, "and the poor become rich." But that is not what he says. The pattern changes and the disciples are told, "the poor have the good news proclaimed to them." While this passage offers much to think about, we can also focus on the meaning of this change in the pattern.

The other actions are miracles that occur because of what Jesus does. Perhaps God is saying that the "solution" to poverty is ultimately going to come more from our own human labors than from God. He is not the one to make the poor rich. Any study indicates that as of now we already have the capacity to feed everyone in the world, so that no one needs to starve. It is not enough for us to keep praying that God help with the poverty in the world. We must take some active role in dealing with it as individuals and communities.

Before all this happens, however, they will seize and persecute you, they will hand you over to the synagogues and to prisons, and they will have you led before kings and governors because of my name. It will lead to your giving testimony. Remember, you are not to prepare your defense beforehand, for I myself shall give you a wisdom in speaking that all your adversaries will be powerless to resist or refute. You will be handed over by parents, brothers, relatives, and friends, and they will put some of you to death. You will be hated by all because of my name, but not a hair on your head will be destroyed. By your perseverance you will secure your lives.

—Luke 21:12-19

The passage contains these predications: they will seize and persecute you, they will hand you over, they will have you led before kings, they will put some of you to death. The predictions of this persecution are not seen as coming from God. The trials of this time will come from others. This is seen in the use of the word "they."

Only once in this passage is the word "I" used: "I myself shall give you a wisdom in speaking." While the suffering of the event will come from others, the strength to get through it will come from God. The difference in the pattern of the language helps remind us that we do not have to always view God as the cause of suffering. Some people presume the bad things in life come directly from God, and that whatever good happens is just accidental. This passage, with its emphasis on a God who helps, shows a God closely involved with caring for those in need.

After six days Jesus took Peter, James, and John and led them up a high mountain apart by themselves. And he was transfigured before them, and his clothes became dazzling white, such as no fuller on earth could bleach them. Then Elijah appeared to them along with Moses, and they were conversing with Jesus. Then Peter said to Jesus in reply, "Rabbi, it is good that we are here! Let us make three tents: one for you, one for Moses, and one for Elijah." He hardly knew what to say, they were so terrified. Then a cloud came, casting a shadow over them; then from the cloud came a voice, "This is my beloved Son. Listen to him." Suddenly, looking around, they no longer saw anyone but Jesus alone with them.

As they were coming down from the mountain, he charged them not to relate what they had seen to anyone, except when the Son of Man had risen from the dead. So they kept the matter to themselves, questioning what rising from the dead meant.

—Mark 9:2-10

At different points in Jesus' ministry we are told that Christ orders those who witness particular events to keep quiet. Examples occur with the ones who witness the healing of the deaf man with the speech impediment (Mark 7:36), the parents who witness their daughter being brought back to life (Luke 8:56), the leper who is cured (Luke 5:14).

These are among some of the people that Jesus commands to keep silent after they are part of a special event. He does the same with those who witness the Transfiguration. But this time his command has changed somewhat. Only at the Transfiguration are they told to keep quiet for a limited period of time, "he charged them not to relate what they had seen to anyone, except when the Son of Man had risen from the dead." Then they are to talk about what happened.

Why at the Transfiguration does he limit their silence only temporarily? A clue can be seen at the end of the story. We are told they questioned what rising from the dead meant.

On Easter Sunday they could break their silence. Jesus wanted them to remember and talk about the event at that time. They did not understand "resurrection." But recalling the Transfiguration might give them a sense that a new life is possible. They saw Moses and Elijah, who had been dead for centuries. The dead can come back to life. Recalling the Transfiguration may have helped them in the days following Easter. Perhaps in God's mind part of the purpose of the Transfiguration was to prepare the apostles for the challenge they would face at the time of the Resurrection.

For us, as for the apostles, there are times when God makes something happen in our lives that will prepare us for challenges in our future. There are times when we look back that perhaps we too can see God's hand in our past. This past event may be something that will help us with a present day challenge. God does help us!

Imagine the Story in Your Mind, Then Ask Questions About What Initially Doesn't Seem to Fit

The stories described throughout Scripture offer us some details about what people said and how they acted. Sometimes lessons can be learned by playing out a story in our mind. Picture how it happened as it is described. At times this can raise questions about some unusual things that occur. Finding an explanation can offer some insights into the event:

> During those days Peter stood up in the midst of the brothers (there was a group of about one hundred and twenty persons in the one place). He said, "My brothers, the scripture had to be fulfilled which the holy Spirit spoke beforehand through the mouth of David, concerning Judas, who was the guide for those who arrested Jesus. He numbered among us and was allotted a share in this ministry. . . . Therefore, it is necessary that one of the men who accompanied us the whole time the Lord Jesus came and went among us, beginning from the baptism of John until the day on which he was taken up from us, become with us a witness to his resurrection." So they proposed two, Joseph called Barsabbas, who was also known as Justus, and Matthias. Then they prayed, "You, Lord, who know the hearts of all, show which one of these two you have chosen to take the place in this apostolic ministry from which Judas turned away to go to his own place." Then they gave lots to them, and the lot fell upon Matthias, and he was counted with the eleven apostles.
>
> —Acts 1:15-17, 21-26

The reading describes the procedure the apostles used so that after the death of Judas their number would return to twelve. It was an important event for them and the early Church. But in the end, having narrowed down the list to two candidates, the person to be called "apostle" is chosen by drawing lots. Why not find some other way to choose someone for this ministry? Drawing lots would seem to be playing a game of chance, as it involves a random selection. Couldn't the eleven have found a better way? At first glance what they did doesn't seem to match the significance of choosing an apostle. Why don't we use lots to determine who serves in important ministries?

The apostles wanted the final selection to be up to God. The prayer they offered shows that they put their faith in God that he would see that the right person joined this ministry. For the apostles, there was nothing random about this at all. Ultimately, it would be God's decision. They began a process which would involve both human and divine effort.

He passed through towns and villages, teaching as he went and making his way to Jerusalem. Someone asked him, "Lord, will only a few people be saved?" He answered them, "Strive to enter through the narrow gate, for many, I tell you, will attempt to enter but will not be strong enough. After the master of the house has arisen and locked the door, then will you stand outside knocking, and saying, 'Lord, open the door for us.' He will say to you in reply, 'I do not know where you are from.' And you will say, 'We ate and drank in your company and you taught in our streets.' Then he will say to you, 'I do not know where [you] are from. Depart from me, all you evildoers!'"

—Luke 13:22-27

If you are in your house and the door is locked and someone knocks on it, how do you decide if you will open it and let that person in? Most of us will decide on the basis of whether or not we know the person. But in this parable, the master of the house doesn't make the decision as we would, but on a very different criteria. Twice he tells the one knocking that his unwillingness to let him in is because he does not know where he comes from. To us that would be irrelevant. What difference does it make where he's from? Why does the master of the house use that as the reason for not allowing him inside?

Perhaps Jesus is reminding us once again that his point of view is different from our own. He doesn't see things quite the way we do. This parable offers us, among other lessons, the reminder that it is important for us to look at what happens around us not only from our own point of view, but also from God's.

On the first day of the Feast of Unleavened Bread, when they sacrificed the Passover lamb, his disciples said to him, "Where do you want us to go and prepare for you to eat the Passover?" He sent two of his disciples and said to them, "Go into the city and a man will meet you, carrying a jar of water. Follow him. Wherever he enters, say to the master of the house, 'The Teacher says, "Where is my guest room where I may eat the Passover with my disciples?"' Then he will show you a large upper room furnished and ready. Make the preparations for us there." The disciples then went off, entered the city, and found it just as he had told them; and they prepared the Passover.

—Mark 14:12-16

By the time Jesus was speaking with the disciples, he had already made arrangements with the master of the house to use his upper room.

Why does Jesus go through this rather elaborate set of directions? Why not just describe the location directly?

The disciples are told to recognize the one they are to follow not by name, but as the one "carrying a water jar." Here we get the impression the disciples would not know his identity. How would this man know who the two disciples were? How was this meeting timed? Would this man be carrying a water jar around, just waiting until the disciples came in?

It would seem Jesus is concerned not only about preparing the room for this last Passover meal with his disciples, but also about preparing the people who would attend. Perhaps this was Jesus' way of showing them that many things about this day would be unusual. The way the room is found; some of the words Jesus would say; the fact that he would be betrayed; what would happen when the meal was over. Things would be different. Their faith would be tested. Logic and reasoning would not be enough. Maybe in part Jesus wanted them to know there would be something different about this time they would spend together. Faith would be required to see it through.

On the evening of that first day of the week, when the doors were locked, where the disciples were, for fear of the Jews, Jesus came and stood in their midst and said to them, "Peace be with you." When he had said this, he showed them his hands and his side. The disciples rejoiced when they saw the Lord. [Jesus] said to them again, "Peace be with you. As the Father has sent me, so I send you." And when he had said this, he breathed on them and said to them, "Receive the holy Spirit. Whose sins you forgive are forgiven them, and whose sins you retain are retained."

—John 20:19-23

Jesus "breathed" on them. Why? It seems like a rather unusual thing to do. Most of us don't go up to people and breathe on them. Perhaps it was his way of showing us that in some of the great events of life, God acts very quietly, in ways that cannot be seen or heard. This can be challenging for us to accept. Often things that are not seen or heard we don't pay much attention to. Perhaps the strongest example of this is the one Jesus uses: breathing. It is usually not noticed, and yet it is one of the very things that keeps us alive.

There are many things God has done for us that we are completely unaware of. Jesus challenges us never to think that when God is quiet, God is gone.

Then he made the disciples get into the boat and precede him to the other side, while he dismissed the crowds. After doing so, he went up on the mountain by himself to pray. When it was evening he was there alone. Meanwhile the boat, already a few miles offshore, was being tossed about by the waves, for the wind was against it. During the fourth watch of the night, he came toward them, walking on the sea. When the disciples saw him walking on the sea they were terrified. "It is a ghost," they said, and they cried out in fear. At once [Jesus] spoke to them, "Take courage, it is I; do not be afraid." Peter said to him in reply, "Lord, if it is you, command me to come to you on the water." He said, "Come." Peter got out of the boat and began to walk on the water toward Jesus. But when he saw how [strong] the wind was he became frightened; and, beginning to sink, he cried out, "Lord, save me!" Immediately Jesus stretched out his hand and caught him, and said to him, "O you of little faith, why did you doubt?" After they got into the boat, the wind died down. Those who were in the boat did him homage, saying, "Truly, you are the Son of God."

—Matthew 14:22-33

In the middle of the storm, Peter gets out of the boat and walks to Jesus on top of the water. Notice though, how close he gets to Jesus before he starts to falter. Matthew says he was close enough that Jesus could catch him by stretching out his hand. Peter was able to get out of the boat and start to walk on the water, but when he gets to within two feet of Jesus, it is then he starts to sink. Why doesn't he sink when he first gets out of the boat? Or why doesn't he sink when he's halfway between the boat and Jesus? Either of those would seem a more likely place to be afraid. Why sink only once he is standing right in front of Christ, where it would seem he would feel the safest?

Perhaps by analogy this is a reminder that sometimes the closer we get to Jesus, the more challenging or difficult our life can become. The more clearly we see him, the more obvious are our own faults. Being close to God can create demands in our life that we never even notice if we keep a safe distance.

The author of the book of Sirach puts it this way: "When you come to serve the LORD, / prepare yourself for trials" (Sir 2:1). Perhaps this is what Luke is referring to when Jesus says, "Much will be required of the person entrusted with much, and still more will be demanded of the person entrusted with more" (Luke 12:48).

Again he left the district of Tyre and went by way of Sidon to the Sea of Galilee, into the district of the Decapolis. And people brought to him a deaf man who had a speech impediment and begged him to lay his hand on him. He took him off by himself away from the crowd. He put his finger into the man's ears and, spitting, touched his tongue; then he looked up to heaven and groaned, and said to him, "Ephphatha!" (that is, "Be opened!") And [immediately] the man's ears were opened, his speech impediment was removed, and he spoke plainly. He ordered them not to tell anyone. But the more he ordered them not to, the more they proclaimed it. They were exceedingly astonished and they said, "He has done all things well. He makes the deaf hear and [the] mute speak."

—Mark 7:31-37

Why did Jesus cure the man in this particular way? Why not just touch the outside of the ear? Why would he put his fingers into the man's ears? Why not just touch his lips or the outside of his mouth? Why put his finger inside the man's mouth to touch his tongue?

Consider what this man would have gone through in his life. At the time there would have been a presumption among some of the people he lived with that this event, like all others, was caused by God. They probably would have thought that either he or his ancestors had done something wrong. He was being punished. Imagine the kind of life he would have had, living with people who were making those kind of judgments about him. This probably would have influenced how they treated him. Some of the people in his town may have avoided him altogether. After all, why take the chance of being with someone that God is punishing? They may have thought God's punishment would also turn to them.

Twenty centuries after this story occurred, we have come to know so much more about the process of healing. This man who was cured needed more than just to have a bone in his ear fixed or some nerve repaired. For genuine healing to occur there were things on the inside that would need to be healed as well. How was he going to start to treat those who had made fun of him? What would he do with the feelings he had for those who were mean to him?

Jesus puts his finger inside the man's ear and mouth perhaps showing that this healing would need to occur on many levels.

Sometimes we think that if someone looks good on the outside, their health is fine. But the world is filled with people who look fine from the outside, but inside have any number of difficulties that show themselves to no one except the individual.

Perhaps part of the message of Jesus in the manner of the cure is to help us realize that we are all more fragile than we think. It's not just our appearance that expresses who we are, but the inside as well.

Sometimes What Is Not Said Is Important Too

We are all familiar with what is meant by the phrase "nonverbal communication." How we gesture, the way we stand, the expression on our face show that we can communicate even when we are not using words. Perhaps the most obvious type of nonverbal communication can be seen by paying attention to what we don't say. We can be conveying ideas to others even by the words we leave out. Not saying something is one way we communicate. This is true with Scripture as well:

> "I am the bread of life. Your ancestors ate the manna in the desert, but they died; this is the bread that comes down from heaven so that one may eat and not die. I am the living bread that came down from heaven; whoever eats this bread will live forever; and the bread that I will give is my flesh for the life of the world."
>
> The Jews quarreled among themselves, saying, "How can this man give us [his] flesh to eat?" Jesus said to them, "Amen, amen, I say to you, unless you eat the flesh of the Son of Man and drink his blood, you do not have life within you. . . ."
>
> As a result of this, many [of] his disciples returned to their former way of life and no longer accompanied him. Jesus then said to the Twelve, "Do you also want to leave?" Simon Peter answered him, "Master, to whom shall we go? You have the words of eternal life."
>
> —John 6:48-53, 66-68

As Jesus offers these challenging words in the Bread of Life discourse, he notices that some of the crowd begin to leave as they find what he is saying difficult to accept. What's interesting is what is not said. Notice that as people are walking away, Jesus never calls them back. He does not explain his teaching in different words, nor does he suggest to the crowd that he is willing to soften his explanation about the importance of this great gift of his Body and Blood. This significant omission is what in part allows the Church to defend its teaching of the "real presence." Since Jesus did not call the people back to teach this any differently (in fact, he even asks the apostles if they are going to leave), we can interpret this passage as an indication that God is truly present in the Eucharist.

> I am the good shepherd. A good shepherd lays down his life for the sheep. A hired man, who is not a shepherd and whose sheep are not his own, sees a wolf coming and leaves the sheep and runs away, and

the wolf catches and scatters them. This is because he works for pay and has no concern for the sheep. I am the good shepherd, and I know mine and mine know me. . . .

—John 10:11-14

There can be several layers of meaning to this teaching where Jesus proclaims himself the "good shepherd." One interpretation is to look at something Jesus doesn't say. By analogy, the "wolf" Jesus speaks of might be compared to something that attacks us in the twenty-first century—not an animal, but anything we find in our life that is difficult to deal with and hurts us. For example, disease, unemployment, famine, natural disasters, Alzheimer's disease, and cancer might be examples of modern day "wolves."

In calling himself the good shepherd Jesus says he will lead the sheep and not leave when the wolf arrives. However, he does not say he will keep the wolf away. Being a follower of Jesus is not a guarantee that God will now protect me from harm. The "wolf" attacks nonbelievers as well as Christians. In this analogy, though, Jesus promises never to leave us regardless of who or what attacks.

And I tell you, ask and you will receive; seek and you will find; knock and the door will be opened to you.

—Luke 11:9

Perhaps a way to show how this passage can be misinterpreted is by an example. A novena is a prayer meant to be repeated over a period of time. Novenas can be a good way of getting us in the habit of prayer and this is not meant to be critical of them, but I have seen pages with a novena prayer that contained this direction at the bottom: "Make 81 copies and leave nine copies in church for each consecutive day. You will receive your intention before the nine days are over, no matter how impossible it may seem."

This kind of advice is based on a flawed interpretation of "ask and you shall receive." The ending to that novena prayer gives the impression that whatever you ask for, within nine days God will do it—no matter what. Think about it: if you could actually make God do something because you put copies of a prayer in church, then you are more powerful than God is. That prayer can't "work" the way it is suggested.

In interpreting that passage it's worth noting what is missing. Jesus does not say, "ask and you will receive what you ask for." All he says is that if we ask, we will receive . . . something. This passage is a reminder to us that there is no such thing as genuine prayer that is wasted. Whenever we pray, something is happening. However, it is wrong to give people the impression from this passage that we can force God to do what we command.

Then one of the elders spoke up and said to me, "Who are these wearing white robes, and where did they come from?" I said to him, "My lord, you are the one who knows." He said to me, "These are the ones who have survived the time of great distress; they have washed their robes and made them white in the blood of the Lamb.
    For this reason they stand before God's throne
        and worship him day and night in his temple.
    The one who sits on the throne will shelter them.
    They will not hunger or thirst anymore,
        nor will the sun or any heat strike them.
For the Lamb who is in the center of the throne will shepherd them
        and lead them to springs of life-giving water,
        and God will wipe away every tear from their eyes."

—Revelation 7:13-17

This act of God wiping away the tears from our eyes holds out for us a special kind of hope. What kind of hope is it?

Someone has been tested for cancer and waits for the results of the test, hoping that the news will be good. That is not the kind of hope that God is offering here. Someone is laid off from work and is hoping that the unemployment will end soon. That is not the kind of hope God is offering here. Two people make a promise to marry and both hope that their life together will not end. That is not the kind of hope God is offering here.

While God would certainly have concern for each of the people involved in these kinds of situations, what God is offering here is something different. We can get a clue from what God doesn't say. While God promises to wipe away tears, God does not promise to alter events so that you will not cry. In fact, if God wipes away tears, the presumption is that you will cry (or there would be no tears to wipe away).

Do you have a memory of being a child and getting hurt? You start to cry and run to your mother. She consoles you and wipes the tears away. Now you may have wished that something might have been done to prevent you from getting hurt in the first place. But once you were hurt, what a difference it made that someone was there.

Catholics have cancer or go through unemployment or divorce with the same frequency as anyone else. We need to look no further than the death of Jesus on the cross to realize that closeness to God doesn't guarantee freedom from suffering. The great hope that God holds out for each of us is that we will never suffer alone. Whatever comes our way, God will be there as well. Among other things, he is there to wipe the tears away. This passage holds out for us the hope that we can have difficulty and yet still have God—both at the same time.

From that time on, Jesus began to show his disciples that he must go to Jerusalem and suffer greatly from the elders, the chief priests, and the scribes, and be killed and on the third day be raised. Then Peter took him aside and began to rebuke him, "God forbid, Lord! No such thing shall ever happen to you." He turned and said to Peter, "Get behind me, Satan! You are an obstacle to me. You are thinking not as God does, but as human beings do."

—Matthew 16:21-27

This part of the Gospel records one of those times when Jesus speaks about the future. He tells his disciples that he will travel to Jerusalem, suffer, die, and rise. This is, of course, exactly what he did.

But when we look at Peter's reaction, he is concerned about the fact that Jesus predicts he will suffer and die. We are told he did not want any such thing to happen to him. But there is something he doesn't say. Peter does not react at all to the fact that Jesus says he will rise. Why doesn't he? After all, we will all die, but at the time not many believed in anything like the Resurrection. Shouldn't the revelation that Jesus would rise have invoked at least as much reaction as the prediction that he would suffer and die?

This passage helps us reflect on our own life. It is difficult to see beyond suffering. Perhaps it was difficult for Peter to see beyond it as well, and so he has no response to Christ's prediction about rising. He is stuck on the notion of suffering. Going through pain or grief of some sort can be like standing with our nose to the wall. All we can see is the wall, and a rather narrow portion of it at that. This is not to suggest that we ignore our suffering or that of others, but to point out that when there is difficulty, then more than ever we need to see the second part of Jesus' prediction—the difficulty won't last forever.

When What Is Described Is Very Specific, Consider Looking at it from a More General Point of View

The Bible gives us a lot of information about Jesus. We know some details about his birth, what he taught, the people he chose as apostles, some of the places to which he traveled, some of the miracles he performed, and how he suffered, died, and rose. But nowhere in the Bible are we told anything about what he looked like. Some writers who have wondered about this lack of detail have suggested that it was no oversight. They feel that we have not been told about his appearance for a reason.

Perhaps it is easier to see Jesus in ourselves and others when there is a certain anonymity about him. Without a clear description, maybe Jesus can be more easily seen when we look into the eyes of our neighbor. It may make it less difficult for us, regardless of our race or nationality, to act in his name and with his personality. We can be so caught up in judging appearances and acting according to what we see that a lack of description can allow us to see Jesus as belonging to us all.

This idea of keeping something more general, rather than being too specific, may be seen when Jesus refers to his mother as "woman" rather than by her name or her relationship to him.

There are times where something can be so specific so as to make it difficult for another to relate to it. This can happen with some of the events in the Bible. When certain stories seem to have no application to our generation or to this century, perhaps seeing them in a more general way will shed some light on their meaning:

> When John heard in prison of the works of the Messiah, he sent his disciples to him with this question, "Are you the one who is to come, or should we look for another?" Jesus said to them in reply, "Go and tell John what you hear and see: the blind regain their sight, the lame walk, lepers are cleansed, the deaf here, the dead are raised, and the poor have the good news proclaimed to them."
>
> —Matthew 11:2-5

This passage presents us with some very specific examples. It can certainly speak to the blind, the lame, lepers, and the deaf. But if none of these conditions describe you, how can you relate to the words? Try stepping back and looking at this story from a more general point of view.

What do the conditions mentioned in this passage have in common? They all present a certain type of challenge or suffering. Now you are at a level everyone can relate to. What is Jesus saying to all those who face challenges? In the first five examples he indicates the condition is removed: the blind regain their sight; the lame walk; lepers are cleansed; the deaf hear; and the dead are raised. Then when it comes to the poor, he observes that they "have the good news proclaimed to them."

These words of Jesus are for anyone who suffers. Perhaps he is telling us that sometimes the challenges or difficulties we face are temporary (in five of his examples the challenge is removed), and other times they will remain (in his sixth example it stays). But regardless, we are never abandoned by God. God is present in the Good News to be proclaimed to all who are in need. Suffering does not mean God has left us.

Blessed be the God and Father of our Lord Jesus Christ, who has blessed us in Christ with every spiritual blessing in the heavens, as he chose us in him, before the foundation of the world, to be holy and blameless before him. In love he destined us for adoption to himself through Jesus Christ, in accord with the favor of his will, for the praise of the glory of his grace that he granted us in the beloved.

—Ephesians 1:3-6

This is part of the second reading used on the feast of the Immaculate Conception, recalling Mary's conception within her mother. It speaks of the spiritual blessings that have been given to others. On this feast this is applied in a very specific way to Mary being conceived without original sin. In interpreting this passage we do not have to go any further. We can look at this idea as it pertains only to her conception. However, it can present other truths as well. We can look for these if we also consider the passage in a way that is not quite as specific.

We can focus not only on the advantage that Mary was given, but in a more general way recognize that everyone has been given some advantage by God. The unique gifts we each possess have their origin in God's goodness. While Mary was given this unique blessing (freedom from original sin), we have been given something as well. It is up to us to determine what that may be, and to use that gift to help build up God's kingdom.

For as it was in the days of Noah, so it will be at the coming of the Son of Man. In [those] days before the flood, they were eating and drinking, marrying and giving in marriage, up to the day that Noah entered the ark. They did not know until the flood came and carried them all away. So will it be [also] at the coming of the Son of Man. Two men will be out in the field; one will be taken, and one will be left. Two women will be grinding at the mill; one will be taken, and one will be left. Therefore, stay awake! For you do not know on which day your Lord will come.

—Matthew 24:37-42

This passage is a reference to two very specific events: the difficulties that surrounded the flood as well as those that will surround the end of the world. Since the flood in Noah's time is already over and since probably none of us alive now will face the end of the world, what does this passage have to do with us? One way to add to its meaning is to look at it in more general terms. Instead of only looking at it as a description of these two specific difficult events, let's look at it in terms of difficulties in general faced by anyone.

In his description of the people at the time of Noah, they are seen as being focused only on the present. They were not looking back nor were they looking forward. They dealt only with the present moment. They were acting as they would on any other day: eating, drinking, and marrying.

We have all heard the expression "live one day at a time." While this advice has helped many people deal with the challenges they face, it seems here Jesus is suggesting that in some situations (as with the people at Noah's time) that is not always the best way to live. Jesus seems critical of their living only "one day at a time."

Perhaps one interpretation of this passage, when applied to difficulties in general, is that sometimes we should look back and sometimes we should look forward.

When we suffer, looking back to a happier time and searching for better memories can help remind us that our life has had its happy times as well. Finding something to look forward to in the future (even if it is seemingly small and not very eventful) can give us a moment for which to strive that will let us see something other than the present difficulty.

While we don't have to make the ideas in a passage more generalized in order to interpret them, sometimes doing so will give us some added thoughts on what God may be saying to us.

When Mary came to where Jesus was and saw him, she fell at his feet and said to him, "Lord, if you had been here, my brother would not have died." When Jesus saw her weeping, . . . he became perturbed and deeply troubled, and said, "Where have you laid him?" They said to him, "Sir, come and see." And Jesus wept. So the Jews said, "See how he loved him." But some of them said, "Could not the one who

opened the eyes of the blind man have done something so that this
man would not have died?"

So Jesus, perturbed again, came to the tomb. It was a cave and a
stone lay across it. Jesus said, "Take away the stone." Martha, the dead
man's sister, said to him, "Lord, by now there will be a stench; he has
been dead for four days." Jesus said to her, "Did I not tell you that if
you believe you will see the glory of God?" So they took away the stone.
And Jesus raised his eyes and said, "Father, I thank you for hearing
me. I know that you always hear me; but because of the crowd here I
have said this, that they may believe that you sent me." And when he
had said this, he cried out in a loud voice, "Lazarus, come out!" The
dead man came out, tied hand and foot with burial bands, and his
face was wrapped in a cloth. So Jesus said to them, "Untie him and let
him go."

—John 11:32-44

This miracle story has some very specific actions that take place in it,
things that would not have been done if Lazarus had not been raised by
Jesus. Focus for a moment on the role of those observers and friends of
Lazarus. Jesus asks two things of them: they are to roll back the stone
and untie Lazarus when he comes out of the tomb. If we only look at
those actions as they pertain to this specific story, then we may be missing some additional ways that God is speaking to us. However, if those
events are taken in a more general sense they give us some further ideas
to think about.

Perhaps we are being called to recognize that our role as Christians is
similar to that of the mourners that day. We are challenged as an individual, family member, parish, or diocese to "roll back the stone" and
help "untie" those who have "died."

Death comes in many forms. Sometimes the real tragedy is not physical
death, but rather the things that die inside us while we still live. Someone
can be dead to their faith, dead to their marriage, dead in their ability to
forgive, and so on. Do we pile up more stones in front of their grave, making it more difficult should anyone ever try to move them? Do we bind the
person up tighter so that they lose even the desire to come back?

When we look at this miracle from a more general point of view, it
presents us with one of the great challenges of Christianity.

A leper came to him [and kneeling down] begged him and said, "If
you wish, you can make me clean." Moved with pity, he stretched
out his hand, touched him, and said to him, "I do will it. Be made

clean." The leprosy left him immediately, and he was made clean. Then, warning him sternly, he dismissed him at once. Then he said to him, "See that you tell no one anything, but go, show yourself to the priest and offer for your cleansing what Moses prescribed; that will be proof for them."

—Mark 1:40-44

Leprosy is a specific medical illness to which most of us cannot relate. What does a story about lepers have to do with twenty-first-century Americans? Actually, it has an important connection. Try this: Don't look at the cure from leprosy as a blessing. Look for a blessing you have been given. Make the story more general and less specific.

With every blessing from God comes a challenge. In this miracle, although the leper was given a great gift, he was also presented with a challenge: "Tell no one anything," Jesus ordered him "sternly." This is true for the leper in the story, but also for us. The blessings we have been given come with a challenge as well. A compassionate helper is challenged with the need to allow him- or herself to be helped by others; a strong athlete may be challenged with trying to remain humble; a hard worker may face the challenge of balancing being a good provider with spending time with his or her spouse and family; someone blessed with a good intellect may be challenged with keeping a strong belief in God.

The healing of the leper can serve as a reminder not just to be aware of the gifts we have been given, but of the challenges each presents.

Again, the kingdom of heaven is like a merchant searching for fine pearls. When he finds a pearl of great price, he goes and sells all that he has and buys it.

—Matthew 13:45-46

This two-sentence parable is one of the shortest Jesus proclaims, and yet it has a significant meaning. We are told this merchant was a kind of collector. He was searching for pearls and willing to pay a large price for them. On the surface, this may not seem like it has much to do with life in twenty-first-century America. How many people do you know that are trying to collect pearls? So let's step back and make what is so specific more general.

Human beings are natural collectors. We save and accumulate things. In and of itself, Jesus isn't saying that is bad. He never seems critical of the merchant. I think instead Jesus is telling us to be careful in life about just what we decide to collect.

The merchant wanted to collect only what was beautiful—pearls. We sometimes make other choices. Have you ever met someone who collected anger? unhappy memories? grudges? past hurts? These are not nearly as beautiful as what the merchant chose to save.

This parable may be a reminder to us to be careful about what we decide to collect in life. It is a challenge to accumulate what is beautiful. Forgiveness, acts of kindness, and mercy are all examples of beautiful pearls. They can cost a lot to save, but after enough time, most people will find the cost worth the effort.

At once the Spirit drove him out into the desert, and he remained in the desert for forty days, tempted by Satan. He was among wild beasts, and the angels ministered to him.

After John had been arrested, Jesus came to Galilee proclaiming the gospel of God: "This is the time of fulfillment. The kingdom of God is at hand. Repent, and believe in the gospel."

—Mark 1:12-15

Mark describes the temptation of Jesus in the desert with very little detail. However, what he does say is significant.

We are told Jesus was in the desert, but that the angels ministered to him. Do these two ideas cancel each other out? After all, how much of a sacrifice is it to be in the desert, but at the same time be taken care of by angels? Even though most of us cannot relate to living in a desert with wild animals, we can still learn from what Jesus went through.

There may be many ideas Jesus wants us to consider from his being tempted. Perhaps one of them is to widen the meaning of what he experienced. For example, to take what Jesus went through and to transfer it to this generation, the "wild beasts" he spends time with might not be animals. Our generation can look at these beasts as domestic violence or poverty or war or any number of issues that can attack our humanity.

Jesus was not afraid to face the beasts he met in the desert. He was "among" them—not looking on from a safe distance as in a zoo. However, he was not alone. Angels were with him. So perhaps one meaning we can see is that we too are called to be among the wild beasts of our society, which means we can't ignore them either. Like Jesus, though, we should not do this alone. We do it with the help of others—whether we call that help the community of our parish or public prayer or any other means at our disposal to fight what attacks us.

See the Bible as the Story of *Your* Life

The Scriptures are not simply a compilation of stories about other people's lives. They provide a story about your own life. This may be one of the most important ideas to understand about God's Word. Be careful not to look at the Bible only as a book that contains accounts of long ago which have to do with people who have long since died. Do not just see it as a book about others. It is also a look into your life: past, present, and future. Jesus hints at this when he says, "I have told you this so that you may not fall away. . . . I have told you this so that when their hour comes you may remember that I told you" (John 16:1, 4).

Some people prefer to dial a number and talk to someone who can predict their future using cards or astronomical signs. Christians, however, look for insights elsewhere. Much of what is in God's Word speaks of your future already. The journey described in the Bible in many ways is going to be your journey. That's why the Bible is timeless and for every generation. Our challenge as we read it is to move from memory to reality!

Be careful not to look at Scripture as a place to go to keep you safe from the reality of life. The Word of God is meant to draw you into it, rather than provide a safeguard from it.

You will be the prophet at some point in your life, as well as the one who hears the words from other prophets. You have been called by God. Sometimes you will follow, other times you will not, but God will not abandon you. You will be rejected and suffer. You will die and rise.

These events were not recorded so that people could feel they can now escape all the challenges faced by those who have gone before them. At least some of what has happened to those in Scripture will happen to you. It is the story of the life of Christians in every generation.

In the gospels, when events happened in Jesus' life, it was not unusual for him to observe that they occurred "in fulfillment of the Scriptures." It is that way with us. Our lives are meant to fulfill some of the Scriptures as well:

> When the sabbath was over, Mary Magdalene, Mary, the mother of James, and Salome bought spices so that they might go and anoint him. Very early when the sun had risen, on the first day of the week, they came to the tomb. They were saying to one another, "Who will roll back the stone for us from the entrance of the tomb?" When they looked up, they saw that the stone had been rolled back; it was very large.
>
> —Mark 16:1-4

As the women make their way to the tomb, they ask one another, "Who will roll back the stone for us?" The stone was the barrier between them and Jesus. When we recall that the Bible is our story, then the questions of Scripture become our own. And so we too can ask, "Who will roll back the stone for us?" The answer should be as remarkable for us as it was for them: The stone is already rolled back! Everyone has equal access to God. We do not have to earn his attention. At every Mass we proclaim, "Lord, I am not worthy." The words are spoken not to make us think that our goal is to achieve worthiness, but rather as a reminder of reality. We are not worthy, and yet we can be joined to the Lord. There are parts of the spiritual life that you do not get by merit. You receive simply because you are aware of God's presence. Nothing needs to separate us from the Lord. The stone has been moved away. Unfortunately, sometimes we are the ones who move it back.

> Or what woman having ten coins and losing one would not light a lamp and sweep the house, searching carefully until she finds it? And when she does find it, she calls together her friends and neighbors and says to them, "Rejoice with me because I have found the coin that I lost."
>
> —Luke 15:8-9

Jesus recalls the theme of being lost and then found. In this same chapter of Luke's Gospel he repeats this theme in his parables of the lost sheep and the prodigal son. But remember that these are not just stories of long ago, they are our own as well. This is a story that has occurred countless times throughout history, including perhaps in our own lives.

We tend to look at being "lost" as the unfortunate part of that story, or rather, our own story. We don't like to be lost. But isn't it necessary to be lost before we can be found?

It's not uncommon for those who reach the end of their life to spend some time in a nursing home, perhaps with hospice care. Gradually we lose things we once had. Perhaps over time we lose the ability to walk or speak, to see or hear or eat. The world encourages us to think that this "lost" time is wasted time. When a eulogy is delivered it is often as if that time in the deceased's life did not even occur. But remember what Jesus says, what is lost is found. As we are leaving this world, God is preparing us for the next. With everything lost, there is something found.

This story is not about a coin. It is about whoever is reading it. Being lost can be your salvation.

> When he disembarked and saw the vast crowd, his heart was moved with pity for them, for they were like sheep without a shepherd. . . . He asked them, "How many loaves do you have? Go and see." And when they had found out they said, "Five loaves and two fish." So he gave orders to have them sit down in groups on the green grass. The people took their places in rows by hundreds and by fifties. Then, taking the five loaves and the two fish and looking up to heaven, he said the blessing, broke the loaves, and gave them to [his] disciples to set before the people; he also divided the two fish among them all. They all ate and were satisfied. And they picked up twelve wicker baskets full of fragments and what was left of the fish. Those who ate [of the loaves] were five thousand men.
>
> —Mark 6:34, 38-44

This is one of the few accounts that is found in each one of the four Gospels. There must have been some important meaning here that the evangelists didn't want forgotten. While there are many levels of significance, each generation can continue to add to the meaning of this story. See yourself in this miracle. The question asked of the disciples is the question put to you: "How many loaves do you have?"

Consider the food that was brought forward: five loaves and two fish. This amount was completely disproportionate to the need. The miracle began with something very small. The amount of food was insignificant to the thousands who were gathered. And yet it was sufficient enough for Jesus to make something great.

Things that are seemingly insignificant can sometimes be the most valuable. The more difficult a person's life is, the more this idea is true. Spending time in a hospital room with a family whose parent is about to die—just standing there even if nothing is spoken—may appear to be so insignificant to the need (a hoped for miracle), and yet can be of great support.

Someone once observed that a person who is drowning doesn't care about the size of the life preserver. You don't have to solve everyone's problems; small things do a great deal, especially to the person most in need.

How many loaves do you have?

Then Herod called the magi secretly and ascertained from them the time of the star's appearance. He sent them to Bethlehem and said, "Go and search diligently for the child. When you have found him, bring me word, that I too may go and do him homage." After their audience with the king, they set out. And behold, the star that they had seen at its rising preceded them, until it came and stopped over the place where the child was. They were overjoyed at seeing the star, and on entering the house they saw the child with Mary his mother. They prostrated themselves and did him homage. Then they opened their treasures and offered him gifts of gold, frankincense, and myrrh.

—Matthew 2:7-11

Understanding the religion a person belongs to can bring about a greater appreciation of that faith. For example, to know what a "sacrament" is and to know what is believed about communion would be important for someone who is practicing the Catholic faith. However important knowledge is to religion, faith must also have a place in the human heart.

When it comes to religion knowledge is of value, but, as in other areas of life, knowing only takes us so far. To remind someone who has lost a loved one in death that in fact the one who is missed is alive with God may increase knowledge, but it does not remove the pain of loss. To explain to a patient the type of cancer that has developed and how it started may make her or him wiser about the disease, but the person will still likely be scared.

We can call the Magi "wise" perhaps because they realized it was not enough for them to know someone special was born, they had to experience what they knew. They had to travel, to see, to adore, to offer gifts. They had to see, hear, and touch the one they knew about.

We are like the Magi, and this is also our story. Their journey can be compared to the one we take to church each weekend. Hopefully it is not enough for us to believe in God and know of God's existence. We must do the same as the Magi. Although our journey is much shorter, it has a similar purpose. At Mass we experience what it is like to hear, see, and touch God. Like the Magi, we move from what it means to know to the deeper realm of experience.

Chapter 5

Reflect

Combining the guidelines offered in Chapters 3 and 4, we turn our attention now to putting these into practice. Let's consider some possible interpretations of different passages from Scripture.

Each passage that follows has three parts: the Scripture passage itself, one possible interpretation, a question for reflection. Each passage from the Bible has a word or phrase that is highlighted in bold text. This highlighting is not found in the Scriptures, but has been done here to make it easier to see what part of the passage has been narrowed down to be the focus of the interpretation.

There is more than one way to interpret each of the sections that have been chosen. The Bible is so filled with meaning that no one could offer a complete enough explanation that would include all possible interpretations of each passage. The goal here is to offer one of many different ways of looking at the verses, not to say it is the only way, or even the best way.

The reflection question provided at the end is important to consider. The Bible is not just a book to be studied, but is also meant to help us live. Reflecting on how God's Word can change my life is necessary in any study of Scripture.

A medical student can study, dissect, and memorize facts about a cadaver. All that is a useful process, but he falls short of being able to breathe life into what is being studied. Our challenge is not just to study the Bible, but to make the Scriptures come alive.

As you read this section, I hope you will come up with other interpretations as well, making it even more evident that God is speaking to you:

> And raising his eyes toward his disciples he said:
> "Blessed are you who are **poor,**
>   for the kingdom of God is yours.

Blessed are you who are now **hungry,**
　　for you will be satisfied.
Blessed are you who are now **weeping,**
　　for you will laugh.
Blessed are you when **people hate you,**
　　and when they exclude and insult you,
　　and denounce your name as evil
　　on account of the Son of Man.
Rejoice and leap for joy on that day!
　　　Behold, your reward
　　will be great in heaven. For their
　　　ancestors treated the prophets
　　in the same way.
But woe to you who are rich,
　　for you have received your consolation.
But woe to you who are filled now,
　　for you will be hungry.
Woe to you who laugh now,
　　for you will grieve and weep.
Woe to you when all speak well of you,
　　for their ancestors treated the false
　　prophets in this way."

　　　　　　　　　　—Luke 6:20-26 (emphasis added)

According to Jesus, the four blessed human conditions are poverty, hunger, tears, and misunderstanding. I don't think Jesus is suggesting that these are specific goals to achieve, but rather to consider what they all have in common: among other characteristics, they are all conditions of imperfection. In a perfect world they would not exist. At times there is a sense in which imperfection is a "blessed" condition.

I think the recovering alcoholic, for example, has opportunities to know and experience God in ways that are profound. I think the same is true about the adulterer who is sorry; the sick patient who is searching; or the person battling an eating disorder. These people, and others like them, have a potential for holiness in the spiritual life that surpasses what some would think. In part this may be because these individuals know exactly what it means to be less than whole . . . to be imperfect.

Pursuit of the spiritual life can soar to greater heights in one who is needy, compared with one who thinks he or she is already filled. The beatitudes remind us that you don't have to be perfect in order to be blessed.

In what area of my life am I imperfect?
Do I accept this as a challenge to grow rather than a reason to fail?

"Stop judging and you will not be judged. Stop condemning and you will not be condemned. Forgive and you will be forgiven. Give and gifts will be given to you; a good measure, packed together, shaken down, and overflowing, will be poured into your lap. For the measure with which you measure will in return be measured out to you." And he told them a parable, "**Can a blind person guide a blind person?** Will not both fall into a pit? No disciple is superior to the teacher; but when fully trained, every disciple will be like his teacher."

—Luke 6:37-40 (emphasis added)

Can a physician with cancer treat a patient with cancer? Yes. Can a dentist with a cavity fix a patient with a cavity? Certainly. Does a recovering alcoholic have something to offer a fellow alcoholic? Yes.

It is a common idea that someone with a difficulty is better able to help someone with the same problem. But Jesus asks whether someone blind can guide someone else who is blind. Here the answer is no.

How is this different from the other situations? The first examples are based on knowledge. The physician knows something about healing; the dentist understands the procedure; the recovering alcoholic has thought through events in his or her life.

But in Jesus' question, something is different. Even though an understanding blind person may be able to help a fellow blind person cope with life, what the blind person needs to walk down the street is not more knowledge. Even if both blind people were once doctors of ophthalmology, their knowledge of the eye will not make it easier to walk.

Jesus would remind us that knowledge and understanding, as important as they are, only go so far. We must be careful not to connect our faith only with what is in our mind. We cannot stop believing just because we don't have all the answers.

How do I react when things become more difficult for me to figure out? What kind of an impact does this have on my religion and faith?

He said, "This is how it is with the kingdom of God; it is as if a man were to scatter seed on the land and would sleep and rise night and day and the seed would sprout and grow, **he knows not how**. Of its own accord the land yields fruit, first the blade, then the ear, then the full grain in the ear. And when the grain is ripe, he wields the sickle at once, for the harvest has come."

—Mark 4:26-29 (emphasis added)

In this passage Jesus presents the analogy of comparing the kingdom of God to a seed. Part way through his idea he admits that even though the seed sower may not understand the process of what's going on inside the seed, it sprouts and grows anyway.

In other words, you don't have to understand the mechanics of how a seed grows in order for the seed to "work." This is true of many things in our world. A passenger can fly in an airplane without understanding what keeps the plane in the air. Someone in an office can send a fax without being able to offer a technical explanation of how the other office receives it.

Perhaps we can even take what Jesus says a step further: maybe sometimes we are better off not understanding.

What profession of people tend to have above average anxiety before undergoing a surgical procedure? One group would be nurses who find themselves on the receiving end of medical care. Why? Because they understand all the things that can go wrong. While some things are important for us to understand, not everything fits into that category.

This idea can be applied to how we deal with God. We should not always be too anxious to replace mystery with security. Even though it may be in our nature to understand and to figure out . . . there are times when this is not going to happen, and times when we need to realize that *not* understanding can still be compatible with our religion and faith.

The one thing about "not knowing" is that sometimes it can still leave room for hope.

Can I accept that God is able to act, even if I don't understand everything?

Then James and John, the sons of Zebedee, came to him and said to him, **"Teacher, we want you to do for us whatever we ask of you."** He replied, "What do you wish [me] to do for you?" They answered him, "Grant that in your glory we may sit one at your right and the other at your left." Jesus said to them, "You do not know what you are asking. Can you drink the cup that I drink or be baptized with the baptism with which I am baptized?" They said to him, "We can." Jesus said to them, "The cup that I drink, you will drink, and with the baptism with which I am baptized, you will be baptized; but to sit at my right or at my left is not mine to give but is for those for whom it has been prepared."

—Mark 10:35-40 (emphasis added)

James and John want Jesus to do whatever they ask of him. Put simply, Jesus says no. All who pray have found themselves in a similar situation. God does not always do whatever we ask.

In this part of the Gospel we are given two hints as to why that is. First, in a way Jesus is telling us to be careful about what we pray for. What at one moment in our lives seems like a good idea might actually create more difficulty if granted. Perhaps God, being aware of this, saves us from a greater problem that as yet we do not see.

There is another reason that sometimes God does not do things our way. Sometimes we pray to God to do something that we should be taking care of. In this account, ultimately it is how we have lived our lives that determines whether we are with God in glory.

It can be so simple at Mass for us to answer, "Lord hear our prayer" to a petition seeking God to root out, for example, social injustice. We might even feel somewhat at peace in our life for having prayed for a worthy cause. But have we done anything to help promote just laws or to vote carefully for good law makers? Yes, God can influence us, but it is also important that we be willing to act as well.

What is one thing I pray for God to do,
while at the same time making no effort myself to work at it as well?
Should I accept some responsibility?

You are the **salt** of the earth. But if salt loses its taste, with what can it be seasoned? It is no longer good for anything but to be thrown out and trampled underfoot. You are the **light** of the world. A city set on a mountain cannot be hidden. Nor do they light a lamp and put it under a bushel basket; it is set on a lampstand, where it gives light to all in the house. Just so, your light must shine before others, that they may see your good deeds and glorify your heavenly Father.

—Matthew 5:13-16 (emphasis added)

There is something about salt and light that we are called to imitate. What do these two things have in common?

If someone has no salt in his or her body, that person cannot sustain life. However, too much salt can also contribute to illness.

When there is no light, we walk blind. But too much light is also blinding. Anyone who has driven a car with the sun shining through the front windshield knows what the glare of sunlight can do.

Light and salt do have something in common: for both of them, either extreme—too much or too little—is damaging.

The encouragement to be salt and light may be seen as a challenge to avoid living at the extremes of life. Examples of this can be found in particular types of thoughts, such as:

- If I make one mistake . . . then I can't do anything right.
- If everyone doesn't like me . . . then I'm no good at making friends.
- If I don't get an "A" for a grade . . . then I'm stupid.
- If I'm not perfect . . . then I'm terrible.
- If I'm not in complete control . . . then I have no control.
- If I'm not in great health . . . then I'm at death's doorstep.
- Someone might even have this way of thinking at a funeral: If you're dead . . . then you no longer live.

It's the right balance of salt and light that promote life. The same is true with how we think. In both cases extremes are often damaging.

Are there any thoughts I have that encourage me to look at my life or another's in ways that are extreme?

John [the Baptist] answered them, "I baptize with water; but **there is one among you whom you do not recognize,** the one who is coming after me, whose sandal strap I am not worthy to untie." This happened in Bethany across the Jordan, where John was baptizing.

The next day he saw Jesus coming toward him and said, "Behold, the Lamb of God, who takes away the sin of the world. He is the one of whom I said, 'A man is coming after me who ranks ahead of me because he existed before me.' **I did not know him** . . . ."

—John 1:26-31 (emphasis added)

In this account John the Baptist makes the comment that others, himself included, failed to recognize Jesus when they saw him. Several years later, when Jesus would appear after the Resurrection, the gospel writers would record a similar experience. There are those who would see Jesus but not recognize him.

Perhaps this is a challenge that people of every generation face. We see people all the time, but do we recognize who they are? I don't mean do we know the person's name, but rather do we know . . . the person? We can observe a person but not have a clue as to what is going on inside.

I'm not suggesting we walk around telling everyone how we feel all the time or everything that is on our mind, but that we allow ourselves to be recognized on at least two occasions:

First, when we are before God. We should be open enough so that we want God to recognize us for who we truly are. Yes, God can do that even when we hide, but there is a value for us in doing it freely. Second, we should usually allow at least one other person to recognize us. Whether we call that person uncle, grandma, mom or dad, spiritual director, husband or wife, counselor, best friend, or confessor, whatever the title, it's good to have at least one person who not only sees us, but recognizes us for who we are.

What is the biggest challenge for me in recognizing who other people are?

In the beginning was the Word,
    and the Word was with God,
    and the Word was God.
He was in the beginning with God.
All things came to be through him,
    and without him nothing came to be.
What came to be through him was life,
    and this life was the light of the human race;
the light shines in the darkness,
    and the darkness has not overcome it.

A man named John was sent from God. He came for testimony, to testify to the light, so that all might believe through him. He was not the light, but came to testify to the light. The true light, which enlightens everyone, was coming into the world.

And **the Word became flesh**
and made his dwelling among us,
and we saw his glory,
the glory as of the Father's only Son,
full of grace and truth.

—John 1:1-9, 14 (emphasis added)

Do you recall hearing talks on Mother's Day that use words like "saints" and "angels" to refer to our mothers, exalting their qualities to a perfect degree? Have you ever been to funerals and heard a homily that talked about the deceased as if he or she had no faults and never had even the slightest moral failure? Sometimes at funerals I think if the deceased could respond, he or she would wonder who is being eulogized.

It may be sentimental to talk about mothers in ways that make it seem as if they do it all and do it perfectly, and maybe that's a part of what Mother's Day is all about, but it's not reality. No one is perfect.

It may be sentimental to talk about the deceased as being so loving and caring that the person had no equal. Maybe that's part of what a funeral is all about, but it's not reality either.

Why do we feel as if there's something degrading about admitting they are human, as human as the rest of us? Perhaps at some point we have come to the conclusion that to be "human" isn't much of a compliment.

Maybe that's why unless some people can look at themselves as "super-human" they think they are less than good. Perhaps that's why there are those concerned about killing a whale but show no interest in the destruction of a human life. It may also explain why some people can look at others and, if they see fault, see someone unworthy of their love.

In this part of John's Gospel we are reminded Jesus became one of us: he became flesh. In doing so, we are challenged to lead the kind life he calls us to. It is ironic that some have lost respect for the very thing that is our claim to fame: we are human.

Do I really try to be good at being human?

During those days Mary set out and traveled to the hill country in haste to a town of Judah, where she entered the house of Zechariah and greeted Elizabeth. When Elizabeth heard Mary's greeting, the infant leaped in her womb, and Elizabeth, filled with the holy Spirit, cried out in a loud voice and said, "Most blessed are you among women, and blessed is the fruit of your womb. And how does this happen to me, that the mother of my Lord should come to me? **For at the moment the sound of your greeting reached my ears, the infant in my womb leaped for joy.** Blessed are you who believed that what was spoken to you by the Lord would be fulfilled."

—Luke 1:39-45 (emphasis added)

For Mary and Elizabeth this was a joyful event: the celebration of new life. But two thousand years later not everyone who hears this kind of a story reacts with happiness, such as:

- the couple having a difficult time conceiving and wondering if they'll ever have a child;
- the person looking back with regret on a decision to have an abortion;
- someone who would like to start a family but can't seem to find the right person to marry;
- the couple who feels the loss of a miscarriage.

For all these people society provides many ways for them to be reminded of their pain:

- walking through a store past racks of baby clothes;
- having a friend or relative announce she's having another child;
- seeing a mother push her child in a stroller;
- and even coming to church and hearing a story about a miraculous and successful birth.

This gospel passage is a reminder to us that a sight that brings happiness to one person can bring sadness to another. We are reminded today that there are few universal signs of happiness. Knowing this and being careful about it is what helps us to form the Christian virtue called compassion—the admission that, in some ways, we experience things so differently from one another. What makes one person happy may bring an opposite feeling to another.

> *Do I go through my day presuming*
> *that everyone experiences reality the same way I do?*
> *If I do, can I think of a time when I might have been wrong to do this?*

He proposed another parable to them. "The kingdom of heaven may be likened to a man who sowed good seed in his field. While everyone was asleep his enemy came and sowed weeds all through the wheat, and then went off. When the crop grew and bore fruit, the weeds appeared as well. The slaves of the householder came to him and said, 'Master did you not sow good seed in your field? Where have the weeds come from?' He answered, 'An enemy has done this.' His slaves said to him, **'Do you want us to go and pull them up?' He replied, 'No,** if you pull up the weeds you might uproot the wheat along with them. Let them grow together until the harvest; then at harvest time I will say to the harvesters, "First collect the weeds and tie them in bundles for burning; but gather the wheat into my barn."'"

—Matthew 13:24-30 (emphasis added)

In this parable the "harvester" is God, the "wheat" can refer to what is good about us, and the "weeds" can refer to what is evil about us. What is interesting is the request of the harvester that the weeds and wheat be allowed to grow together. Haven't we been taught that as Christians our goal should be to get rid of the weeds, i.e., what is evil? For the time being, why does Jesus not want them separated from the wheat?

Perhaps he recognizes that it may not always be easy for the two to be distinguished. For example, sometimes as we grow and live out our life, what we experience as a strong positive characteristic (wheat) ends up later in life becoming a weed. And sometime what we think is a weed is actually wheat in disguise.

Another example of this occurs for most of us when we sin. Prior to sin most people will allow their mind to play a trick on them. They will see some good or some reward in what they are about to do, even though what they are doing is sinful. What is actually a weed (the sin) is perceived by the mind to be wheat.

Jesus' caution is to be careful so that in the process the good is not destroyed unknowingly. Perhaps we need the help of the harvester to tell the two apart.

How has distinguishing the weeds from the wheat of my life
been confusing at times?

> Then the Pharisees went off and plotted **how they might entrap him** in speech. They sent their disciples to him, with the Herodians, saying, "Teacher, we know that you are a truthful man and that you teach the way of God in accordance with the truth. And you are not concerned with anyone's opinion, for you do not regard a person's status. Tell us, then, what is your opinion: Is it lawful to pay the census tax to Caesar or not?" Knowing their malice, Jesus said, "Why are you testing me, you hypocrites? Show me the coin that pays the census tax." Then they handed him the Roman coin. He said to them, "Whose image is this and whose inscription?" They replied, "Caesar's." At that he said to them, "Then repay to Caesar what belongs to Caesar and to God what belongs to God." When they heard this they were amazed, and leaving him they went away.
>
> —Matthew 22:15-22 (emphasis added)

The Pharisees were anxious to have the respect of the people. They wanted others to believe in them and follow their ideas. But in this passage they go a step further. They are asking Jesus this question in order to trip him up, hoping that he would be confused or give some controversial answer.

For this group, it was not enough for them that they be successful, they also wanted Jesus to *fail*. Those are two different goals.

Although it's not likely we'd say it out loud, sometimes in moments of insecurity we are capable of taking that same approach. It starts with a way of thinking about relationships we are in:

- It's not enough that you like me, I want you to dislike this particular person.
- It's not enough that I succeed, I want you to fail.
- It's not enough that you're kind to me, you need to be mean to this individual.

In the Scriptures the Pharisees are sometimes portrayed as acting in this way. What allows us to act differently is to realize that I can be successful, and if others are successful too, that doesn't make me less so. I can have a friend, and if someone enjoys that person's company too, that doesn't make them less of a friend to me.

Some of the Pharisees couldn't learn these kinds of lessons, and were anxious to see Jesus fail. Being aware of what they tried, hopefully we will be more careful not to do the same to others.

Am I very good at sharing friendships and success with others?

The Jews quarreled among themselves, saying, "How can this man give us [his] flesh to eat?" Jesus said to them, "Amen, amen, I say to you, unless you eat the flesh of the Son of Man and drink his blood, you do not have life within you. Whoever eats my flesh and drinks my blood has eternal life, and I will raise him on the last day. For my flesh is true food, and my blood is true drink. **Whoever eats my flesh and drinks my blood remains in me and I in him.** Just as the living Father sent me and I have life because of the Father, so also the one who feeds on me will have life because of me.

—John 6:52-57 (emphasis added)

Most people want to have some recognition that as an individual they matter, and so early in life we determine a kind of "identity niche." A child who already has a brother or sister will sometimes establish an identity different from that of other family members. Doing this establishes one person as unique from his or her siblings. This helps to account for children in the same family being so different.

There are two concerns with this process though. The first is that if the person feels no worthwhile quality or ability to distinguish him or her from others in the family, then that child may begin choosing something negative by which to become known.

However, even good and positive identities can be cause for concern. For example, if early on a person chooses the identity of a "helper," that individual may derive a sense of personal worth and support from that identity. As the person grows, there may even be a challenge that is accepted to always keep things in that role: I am the helper . . . others are the ones who need help. Such a person might not tell others his or her own needs and might find it difficult to ask someone else for help, as that would mean a reversal of roles.

There are many people who are kind and helpful to others, but find in spirituality a particular type of challenge. If they view their own sense of worth from their ability to help, then they may find it difficult to be genuinely in need of God.

The Eucharist and the Scriptures are two of the many ways in which Christ allows us to touch him. We need to remember to be open enough to allow him to touch us.

Am I as good at allowing others to help me, as I am at helping others?

When they had finished breakfast, Jesus said to Simon Peter, "Simon, son of John, do you love me more than these?" He said to him, "Yes, Lord, you know that I love you." He said to him, "Feed my lambs." He then said to him a second time, "Simon, son of John, do you love me?" He said to him, "Yes, Lord, you know that I love you." He said to him, "Tend my sheep." He said to him the third time, "Simon, son of John, do you love me?" Peter was distressed that he had said to him a third time, "Do you love me?" and he said to him, **"Lord, you know everything; you know that I love you."** [Jesus] said to him, "Feed my sheep."

—John 21:15-17 (emphasis added)

After being asked three times "Do you love me?" Peter becomes frustrated. He feels he shouldn't have to say out loud what he is confident Jesus already knows. Peter takes a view that many others would take: since you know it in your mind, it doesn't need to be spoken. But as happens so often, Jesus has a different idea. For Peter and for us, Jesus says that sometimes it is not enough that an idea be in someone's mind, it should still be spoken out loud.

And so while some might say to their husband or wife, "You know I love you. I work and support our family as best I can. That shows how I feel," Jesus might say those kinds of positive feelings should still be put into words.

Someone might suggest, "I don't need to go to confession, God knows my sins and he knows I'm sorry. I don't need to say anything out loud." Jesus might have a different idea.

Another person might presume, "I don't have to sing or pray when I come to Mass. God knows I care. It's enough that I'm here." Jesus would suggest the importance of saying things out loud anyway.

A person can make an appointment with a priest to discuss a problem. The individual is composed at the beginning. But as soon as the person says out loud what is causing the pain, emotions change and tears begin to flow. Saying something out loud makes it real. It applies when we go to confession as well as in everyday life.

Whether we deal with God or each other, there are some things which are best spoken out loud.

What kind of things in my life contribute to making it more difficult for me to put my feelings into words—either with a friend, spouse, or God?

While the crowd was pressing in on Jesus and listening to the word of God, he was standing by the Lake of Gennesaret. He saw two boats there alongside the lake; the fisherman had disembarked and were washing their nets. Getting into one of the boats, the one belonging to Simon, he asked him to put out a short distance from the shore. Then he sat down and taught the crowds from the boat. After he had finished speaking, he said to Simon, "Put out into deep water and lower your nets for a catch." Simon said in reply, "Master, **we have worked hard all night and have caught nothing,** but at your command I will lower the nets." When they had done this, they caught a great number of fish and their nets were tearing. They signaled to their partners in the other boat to come to help them. They came and filled both boats so that they were in danger of sinking.

—Luke 5:1-7 (emphasis added)

By profession some of the apostles were fishermen. That's how they made their living. And yet, at least in the pages of the Bible, they don't seem to be able to catch many fish without Jesus' help. Since they made their living at this though they must have at least been good fishermen, but apparently they were not perfect at what they did.

Sometimes we need to remind ourselves of what the apostles may have recognized: being imperfect is not the same as being terrible. As Christians we are not called to live our lives as if there were only two extremes: perfect or awful. The reality is there are all kinds of points in between the two.

The apostles learned a lesson that's valuable for us as well. For many people in many professions, you don't have to be perfect in order to be good.

*When I try my hardest, are others still unrealistic
in their expectations of what I am able to do in my life?
How do I deal with how they treat me?*

One of the scribes, when he came forward and heard them disputing and saw how well he had answered them, asked him, "Which is the first of all the commandments?" Jesus replied, "This is the first: 'Hear, O Israel! The Lord our God is Lord alone! You shall **love the Lord** your God with all your heart, with all your soul, with all your mind, and with all your strength.' The second is this: 'You shall **love your neighbor** as yourself.' There is no other commandment greater than these."

—Mark 12:28-31 (emphasis added)

Jesus tells us the first focus of our love is not turned inward, but rather is directed toward another, the one we call God. Jesus tells us the second focus of our love is not turned inward, but rather is directed toward others, the ones we call our neighbors. Jesus is not telling us to ignore ourselves, but is reminding us that love naturally moves outward to others. To make this happen, though, presents different challenges.

For example, when parents suffer with disappointment because of something that occurs in the life of some member of the family, they may forget that while they themselves as parents are in pain, it is the other person, the son or daughter in the family, who's actually going through the difficulty.

It may be one thing to feel pain because something has gone wrong in the life of someone you care about, but it is usually much worse if you're the one going through it. Sometimes we can become so consumed with a situation that the concern we have starts to be directed only inward, rather than trying to support and understand the one going through the difficulty.

Human beings have only a limited amount of energy to spend on love. The insight of Jesus is to spend a good part of it focusing not only on ourselves, but others as well.

*Do I find myself getting caught up in how I feel and in what I'm going through
when someone I care about is suffering?*

They came to Jericho. And as he was leaving Jericho with his disciples and a sizable crowd, Bartimaeus, a blind man, the son of Timaeus, sat by the roadside begging. On hearing that it was Jesus of Nazareth, he began to cry out and say, "Jesus, son of David, have pity on me." And many rebuked him, telling him to be silent. But he kept calling out all the more, "Son of David, have pity on me." Jesus stopped and said, "Call him." So they called the blind man, saying to him, "**Take courage;** get up, he is calling you." He threw aside his cloak, sprang up, and came to Jesus. Jesus said to him in reply, "What do you want me to do for you?" The blind man replied to him, "Master, I want to see." Jesus told him, "Go your way; your faith has saved you." Immediately he received his sight and followed him on the way.

—Mark 10:46-52 (emphasis added)

Bartimaeus had heard who Jesus was. He would have been hoping that he would do something to help, and so he is not shy about calling out his name. Jesus stops and calls him to come forward. His followers deliver the happy news that Jesus will see him, but they begin with the phrase "Take courage." Why say that? Is it possible that for a moment Bartimaeus was afraid? If he was it didn't last long, because we are told he *"sprang up"* and went to Jesus. But it seems like, just for a split second, there was some indecision on his part, and he needed to be encouraged.

Perhaps faced with finally being able to see, he wondered, "I'm so used to being blind. I know just what to expect from people: those who care about me and those who shun me. I know how people will treat me. If you take all that away, what will happen?"

I think people in distress find themselves, even if for a moment, facing that same kind of challenge. An alcoholic may wonder, "If I stop drinking what will my life be like? How will I act? This is the only way I know how to be."

Like Bartimaeus we can for a moment be afraid to leave behind part of our identity, especially if it involves ways we have used to cope with life's difficulties. Jesus tells us what the followers of Christ told the blind man: "Take courage."

Do I let fear keep me from improving who I am?

The apostles gathered together with Jesus and reported all they had done and taught. He said to them, "**Come away by yourselves to a deserted place** and rest a while." People were coming and going in great numbers, and they had no opportunity even to eat. So they went off in a boat by themselves to a deserted place. People saw them leaving and many came to know about it. **They hastened there on foot from all the towns and arrived at the place before them.**

—Mark 6:30-33 (emphasis added)

Jesus and the apostles had no time even to eat. Jesus' idea is that they will get into this boat and go to a deserted place so that they will all be able to rest for a while. That's his plan, but it does not work out that way at all. They find that when they get to the shore, there are all kinds of people there who arrived before they did. Things did not turn out the way Jesus wanted them to. This happens every so often in the Gospels; Jesus wants one thing and something else happens.

Perhaps this allows us to question whether all things that occur turn out the exact way God wants them to. This passage would suggest they do not. The most obvious example is sin. Would it make any sense every time we sin for God to be thinking, "I want you to sin." God gives us tremendous freedom and it is not usually taken away.

How often during a tragedy do some people throw around the phrase, "It's God's will"? If by saying that they mean that God wanted the tragedy to occur just as it did, then I don't know how they are able to come to that conclusion with any certainty. If that's not what they mean, then perhaps they should find some other way to express their sympathy.

This passage doesn't hold out for us the criteria to know what is or isn't divine will, but it does suggest that not everything happens exactly the way God would like it to.

How do I deal with God when difficulty strikes my life?
What role do I think God plays in the suffering I have experienced?

When Jesus finished all these words, he said to his disciples, "You know that in two days' time it will be Passover, and the Son of Man will be handed over to be crucified." Then the chief priests and the elders of the people assembled in the palace of the high priest, who was called Caiaphas, and **they consulted together to arrest Jesus by treachery and put him to death**. But they said, "Not during the festival, that there may not be a riot among the people."

—Matthew 26:1-5 (emphasis added)

Jesus brought peace to the lives of many people. He cured the sick, taught, proclaimed, and gave an example of how to live. And yet there were those who wanted him dead. What explains their malice? There may be many reasons behind their drive to ruin Jesus, but one in particular demonstrates an approach they took.

Most of the things people do or say can have many different interpretations behind them. When Jesus lived there were people who consistently took whatever was the worst interpretation they could come up with. That's what they decided explained Jesus' motive.

When Jesus would cure on the Sabbath, they wouldn't take a good interpretation (Jesus did this because he cared for people); they would take the worst interpretation (it was because he had no regard for custom or the law of Moses).

When Jesus spoke about the kingdom, it wasn't because he was interested in spreading God's love to the world; it was (they concluded) because he wanted a political kingdom established to rival the current one.

This was the pattern some people followed. It is a dangerous way of thinking, however, that can still be found today. For example, partners in troubled relationships tend to see hurts, even minor ones, as intentional—something done to them on purpose—while viewing acts of kindness as accidental. People in more fulfilling relationships display almost the exact opposite pattern of thinking. They generously give credit to the other for any act of kindness, and will go overboard to be understanding when they feel hurt or slighted.

Not only can we do this with each other, but this Scripture passage reminds us we can also do it with God.

Am I too quick to come to the worst interpretation of what I see in others?

Then the kingdom of heaven will be like ten virgins who took their lamps and went out to meet the bridegroom. Five of them were foolish and five were wise. The foolish ones, when taking their lamps, brought no oil with them, but the wise brought flasks of oil with their lamps. Since the bridegroom was long delayed, they all became drowsy and fell asleep. At midnight, there was a cry, "Behold, the bridegroom! Come out to meet him!" Then all those virgins got up and trimmed their lamps. The foolish ones said to the wise, "Give us some of your oil, for our lamps are going out." But the wise ones replied, "**No, for there may not be enough for us and you**. Go instead to the merchants and buy some for yourselves." While they went off to buy it, the bridegroom came and those who were ready went into the wedding feast with him. Then the door was locked. Afterwards, the other virgins came and said, "Lord, Lord, open the door for us!" But he said in reply, "Amen, I say to you, I do not know you." Therefore, stay awake, for you know neither the day nor the hour."

—Matthew 25:1-13 (emphasis added)

In refusing to give some of their oil to the ones who were running out of their own supply, Jesus is not suggesting that being selfish is a virtue. But he is suggesting instead that taking care of your own needs can at times be a priority.

Have you ever known parents who wanted very much to have their son or daughter baptized into the Catholic faith, while they themselves had no desire to ever practice that same faith? By using this analogy of the oil and the lamps, one of the lessons Jesus may want us to consider is that it is the salvation of our own soul that is our first priority—not the salvation of others.

Accepting responsibility for ourselves is used in other organizations as well. If you've traveled on airplanes you may recall the directions given by the flight attendant before the plane takes off. You are reminded that in the event that the main cabin loses air pressure, a mask will fall from a compartment above you. You should put the mask on and oxygen will flow so you can breathe. Then, one particular circumstance is addressed by the attendant. If you are with a child or someone not capable of doing this, whose mask are you to put on first? All the airlines will say the same thing: put your mask on first and then help others do the same.

The parable of Jesus can be a reminder of the responsibility we each have to take care of certain needs of our own. This is not because of selfishness, but rather because you cannot pass onto someone else what you yourself do not have.

Do I accept responsibility for my own growth in the faith
or am I always worried about someone else's?

On the evening of that first day of the week, when the doors were locked, where the disciples were, for fear of the Jews, Jesus came and stood in their midst and said to them, "Peace be with you." When he had said this, **he showed them his hands and his side**. The disciples rejoiced when they saw the Lord.

—John 20:19-21 (emphasis added)

Jesus died a painful and humiliating death. And yet, it is not uncommon when he appears to people after the Resurrection that he makes a point of showing them his hands and his side. Jesus shows his wounds. Perhaps he felt this was a way of identifying himself to others, showing them that it was really Jesus.

Whatever his motive for showing his wounds, it is an action that at times we should imitate. We come before God in our brokenness. It is one of the things that brings us to God. There are times when we, like Jesus, should show our own wounds to another. The sacrament of reconciliation is an ideal time to do as Jesus did.

Christ offers us an example of finding the right time to show our wounds rather than hide them.

How do I deal with my own wounds?
What can the way Jesus acted teach me?

Then he said to them, "Nation will rise against nation, and kingdom against kingdom. There will be powerful earthquakes, famines, and plagues from place to place; and awesome sights and mighty signs will come from the sky.

"Before all this happens, however, they will seize and persecute you, they will hand you over to the synagogues and to prisons, and they will have you led before kings and governors because of my name. It will lead to your giving testimony. Remember, you are not to prepare your defense beforehand, for I myself shall give you a wisdom in speaking that all your adversaries will be powerless to resist or refute. You will even be handed over by parents, brothers, relatives, and friends, and they will put some of you to death. You will be hated by all because of my name, **but not a hair on your head will be destroyed.**"

—Luke 21:10-18 (emphasis added)

Four of the more painful feelings that a human being can experience are betrayal, loneliness, fear of death, and being hated. Jesus takes these four feelings and tells his disciples, if you follow me and do what I ask, all these will be yours. Jesus was very realistic. What he described is how it turned out for many of his followers.

But then at the end of the passage, after having described what would be in their future, he proclaims, "not a hair on your head will be destroyed." But how is that consistent with everything he just said was going to happen—the imprisonment, persecution, and death?

One of the themes of Jesus' preaching is that ultimately good will win out over evil. He teaches it in the Beatitudes (blessed are the hungry . . . the hated . . . the persecuted . . .) as well as other places. This idea is repeated here as well. To be sure people can hurt you and cause you to suffer, but to ultimately destroy is beyond their ability. Our perseverance is rewarded. Jesus is not just being realistic about the difficulties his followers will face, but also about what finally awaits those who are faithful.

Do I make efforts to avoid following Jesus when it will put me in a situation where I may suffer or face persecution for standing up for what I believe in?

> Then the scribes and the Pharisees brought a woman who had been caught in adultery and made her stand in the middle. They said to him, "Teacher, this woman was caught in the very act of committing adultery. Now in the law, Moses commanded us to stone such women. So what do you say?" They said this to test him, so that they could have some charge to bring against him. Jesus bent down and began to write on the ground with his finger. But when they continued asking him, he straightened up and said to them, "Let the one among you who is without sin be the first to throw a stone at her." Again he bent down and wrote on the ground. And in response, **they went away one by one,** beginning with the elders. So he was left alone with the woman before him. Then Jesus straightened up and said to her, "Woman, where are they? Has no one condemned you?" She replied, "No one, sir." Then Jesus said, "Neither do I condemn you. Go [and] from now on do not sin anymore."
>
> —John 8:3-11 (emphasis added)

The townspeople got what they wanted. They caught this woman in adultery, the penalty for her was death. They were willing to kill her. They planned to force her out of the city, form a circle around her, and pick up the stones. Then everything changed. The result turned out to be very different from how the story started. The woman didn't die, and it was the crowd that walked away in shame. The members of this crowd attempted to get what they wanted, but the end result was very different from what they expected.

Sometimes when we try too hard to make what we want come true, we discover the same result: things turn out differently than what we had thought. Some people wish for their life to be free of work and care, but then when they retire and their dream comes true, they say they are bored. Some people wish their life would slow down so at least they could have time to think. But there are those who say one of their biggest difficulties in life is that they have too much time to think. Some people are unhappy in marriage, want to get out, but when they do they sometimes find out that the grass is not greener on the other side. There can be times when we try too hard to take charge of our lives, only to find when we get what we want, our expectations still aren't reached.

One of the lessons we can learn from the townspeople is that there can be times when we are better off not trying to control everything.

How do I deal with events not going the way I want them to?

Then many of his **disciples** who were listening said, "This saying is hard; who can accept it?" Since Jesus knew that his disciples were murmuring about this, he said to them, "Does this shock you? What if you were to see the Son of Man ascending to where he was before? It is the spirit that gives life, while the flesh is of no avail. The words I have spoken to you are spirit and life. But there are some of you who do not believe." Jesus knew from the beginning the ones who would not believe and the one who would betray him. And he said, "For this reason I have told you that no one can come to me unless it is granted him by my Father."

As a result of this, many [of] his disciples returned to their former way of life and no longer accompanied him.

—John 6:60-66 (emphasis added)

Saint John places this discussion after Jesus instructs the crowd to "eat the flesh of the Son of Man and drink his blood" (John 6:53). However, although people in the crowd had questions, at least in this part of the Gospel, it is the reaction of some of his disciples that is presented. These were not people hostile to Jesus, and yet we are told that many of them would no longer accompany him.

As a Church we put an emphasis on bringing our faith to new members, and preaching to those who have not yet heard what God has done. This passage, however, gives us an additional responsibility. We must still continue to actively look after those who currently follow their faith. Being a disciple today is not a guarantee that you will stay a disciple tomorrow. Some of those who followed Jesus one day left him the next. This happens to modern day disciples as well.

Our religious life can be as fragile as our physical life. The responsibility I am talking about is not just that church ministers continue to feed their congregations, but just as important, that each person who practices the faith realizes his and her own obligation to safeguard and grow strong in it. Genuinely participating in the public worship of the Mass and taking an active role in the parish to which you belong are good ways that help keep this gift of faith alive and active.

Do I take my faith for granted?
Do I see it as the gift that it is?

He proposed another parable to them. "The kingdom of heaven may be likened to **a man who sowed good seed** in his field. While everyone was asleep his enemy came and sowed weeds all through the wheat, and then went off. When the crop grew and bore fruit, the weeds appeared as well. The slaves of the householder came to him and said, 'Master did you not sow good seed in your field? Where have the weeds come from?' He answered, 'An enemy has done this.' His slaves said to him, 'Do you want us to go and pull them up?' He replied, 'No, if you pull up the weeds you might uproot the wheat along with them. Let them grow together until the harvest; then at harvest time I will say to the harvesters, "First collect the weeds and tie them in bundles for burning; but gather the wheat into my barn."'"

He proposed another parable to them. "The kingdom of heaven is like **a mustard seed that a person took and sowed in a field**. It is the smallest of all the seeds, yet when full-grown it is the largest of plants. It becomes a large bush, and the 'birds of the sky come and dwell in its branches.'"

He spoke to them another parable. "The kingdom of heaven is like **yeast that a woman took** and mixed with three measures of wheat flour until the whole batch was leavened."

—Matthew 13:24-33 (emphasis added)

These three parables are all describing something about the kingdom of heaven. Not one of them says the kingdom is a church building; rather, it is described in terms of the everyday events of its listeners: preparing bread and planting seed.

This serves as a reminder that God's kingdom is meant to be built up in the circumstances of everyday life: among family, at school, with co-workers.

While participation at Mass is so important, it is not enough. The practice of our faith cannot be limited to a short period of time once a week. Our faith involves less an activity and more of a lifestyle, a way of looking at reality that is so much a part of us that it goes wherever we go. Yes, certainly to church, but also everywhere else.

Am I contributing something with my life to help build up God's kingdom?

Thomas, called Didymus, one of the Twelve, was not with them when Jesus came. So the other disciples said to him, "We have seen the Lord." But he said to them, "Unless I see the mark of the nails in his hands and put my finger into the nailmarks and put my hand into his side, I will not believe." Now a week later his disciples were again inside and

Thomas was with them. Jesus came, although the doors were locked, and stood in their midst and said, "Peace be with you." Then he said to Thomas, "Put your finger here and see my hands, and bring your hand and put it into my side, and do not be unbelieving, but believe." Thomas answered and said to him, "My Lord and my God!"

—John 20:24-28

The phrase "doubting Thomas" has its origin with this passage. But it is not completely accurate to characterize Thomas in that way. In an earlier section of John's Gospel Jesus makes a prediction to those listening and says that he is going to go to Jerusalem to suffer and die. Apparently there must have been some discussion with people asking him not to go, because it is Thomas alone who steps forward and offers his own life saying, "Let us also go to die with him" (John 11:16). In so many words Thomas told Jesus if you are going to die, I won't leave you alone. They can take my life too.

Thomas didn't doubt everything. He did not doubt that suffering and death were real. He did not doubt that there would be difficulty in his vocation as a follower of Jesus. He was willing to go and die with Christ. But when he hears Jesus has risen—*then* he doubts. Saint Thomas did not doubt there would be suffering. His doubt was that there could be a new life without it.

Some of us are "selective" doubters, like Thomas. We don't doubt the suffering. We doubt it can be any different.

The alcoholic who looks in the mirror and just accepts this is how things will be, or the person with the eating disorder who thinks it can never be any better, or the one who has buried a parent or spouse and is convinced happiness can never return—these are all people like Thomas: having no doubt in the suffering, but doubting they will ever see it leave.

Jesus reminded Thomas that you don't have to wait until you die before you have a new life. It was while Thomas was still very much alive that he discovered he could believe.

> *When I see someone who doubts like Saint Thomas,*
> *do I bring them further down or do I offer them hope?*

On the first day of the week, Mary of Magdala came to the tomb early in the morning, while it was still dark, and saw the stone removed from the tomb. So she ran and went to Simon Peter and to the other disciple whom Jesus loved, and told them, "They have taken the Lord from the tomb, and we don't know where they put him." So Peter and the other disciple went out and came to the tomb. They both ran, but the other disciple ran faster than Peter and arrived at the tomb first; he bent down and saw the burial cloths there, but did not go in. When Simon Peter arrived after him, he went into the tomb and saw the burial cloths there, and the cloth that had covered his head, not with the burial cloths but rolled up in a separate place. Then the other disciple also went in, the one who had arrived at the tomb first, and **he saw and believed**. For they did not yet understand the scripture that he had to rise from the dead. Then the disciples returned home.

—John 20:1-9 (emphasis added)

On Easter Sunday morning they go to the tomb and find it empty. It is in the emptiness that they found God.

When children play "hide and seek" the criteria they use to determine where to hide is the one place they think no one will look. In a sense God did the same. What's the last place we expect to find God? Emptiness. We see God much more easily in the full and joyful times of life. While God's presence is certainly there, the greater challenge is to find God when things aren't quite so full or joyful. This is not suggesting that these difficult times are caused by God, but it is to say that God is there.

Death, for example, is an experience of emptiness. A loved one's voice is heard no longer and the deceased is taken from our sight. But if we think that God has also gone since we have lost someone we care about, then we have given up more than the person who died.

God can be found to dwell in many places. Who are we to limit God? We face a challenge similar to the apostles. Can we see and feel emptiness, and yet still believe?

How do I live up to the challenge of finding God in emptiness?

[Jesus said,] "**Which of you wishing to construct a tower does not first sit down and calculate the cost to see if there is enough for its completion?** Otherwise, after laying the foundation and finding himself unable to finish the work the onlookers should laugh at him and say, 'This one began to build but did not have the resources to finish.'"

—Luke 14:28-30 (emphasis added)

This parable is not meant to provide a lesson in financial responsibility, but rather serves as a reminder about our spiritual lives. In telling us that we have to count the cost, Jesus is reminding us that there is a price to pay.

Religion and faith were never just meant to shield us from reality. There is a cost for being involved in matters of faith. This part of the Gospel is saying that believing in God will not keep us from the challenges that everyone faces. We do have a price to pay, although not a monetary one.

While there is no universal list of what everyone must expect to receive in life, Jesus is encouraging us to consider in advance what some of the challenges are. For example, part of the cost will be remaining with God even in the face of trial. A list of some of the trials many people face might include: that at some point a loved one will die, that at times you will be lonely (after all, Jesus says in other places that this is not our home, heaven is), that eventually you will be part of an event where you do not understand at all why it is happening, that a time will come when you will face a trial with your own health. In order to predict a cost, you have to have at least some idea of what to expect. There are those who will conclude that if these things happen, it means God has abandoned them. Can you go through experiences such as these and still believe?

Am I willing to pay a price for being a follower of Christ?

> Gird your loins and light your lamps and be like servants who await their master's return from a wedding, ready to open immediately when he comes and knocks. Blessed are those servants whom the master finds vigilant on his arrival. Amen, I say to you, he will gird himself, have them recline at table, and proceed to wait on them. And should he come in the second or third watch and find them prepared in this way, blessed are those servants. Be sure of this: if the master of the house had known the hour when the thief was coming, he would not have let his house be broken into. You also must be prepared, for **at an hour you do not expect, the Son of Man will come**.
>
> —Luke 12:35-40 (emphasis added)

Given the context of this passage, the admonition Jesus gives at the end of this teaching has something to do with our final moments on earth. Most obviously it can mean that your life will end at a time when you don't expect. However, there is another way we can look at the arrival of the Son of Man.

It is ironic that some people have an easier time attributing difficulty and challenges as coming from God, while they are hesitant to see good and helpful things as coming from God's hand. To interpret this only as

God telling us it is important to be prepared because death will come when you don't expect may keep us from seeing another side to what this passage might mean. What if Jesus wants us to know that when we don't expect it, God will come to help. Not only as our life comes to an end is God there to help us, but in other challenging times as well.

God's being active doesn't always have to be seen as the one who cuts short our lives. God can be seen as the one who will not let us be alone as we pass from this world to the next. God is the one who can help those who remain to face what has happened. In some way, often not known until after the event has occurred, God can help the family even prepare for the challenges they are about to face. And so, God's coming at a time we do not expect can be good news as well, rather than just something to fear.

Do I very often attribute the good things I see in the world as coming from God?

Conclusion

The first recorded question that God asks a human being is, "Where are you?" (Gen 3:9). It seems that from the start God has been looking for us. Throughout history God has left us so many places where God can be found, not the least of which are in the words of Scripture. For many people, these words are proclaimed and reflected on as they participate in the liturgy each weekend.

In the early centuries of the Church Mass was celebrated only one day a week—the Lord's day. This one day was chosen, as it was the day of Jesus' resurrection. Gathering the community together gave everyone a chance to proclaim that even though individually some of their lives were difficult and some would have been experiencing pain or persecution, that Jesus still lived! This is the same proclamation we make as a Church in the twenty-first century. Although there is suffering and turmoil in the world, we want to make it evident to all that we have not been abandoned by God. What better time to do this than on the day when Jesus himself rose and conquered death. By taking time to gather together and meet our Lord again, we send a signal to the world that suffering is not the final victor.

Our truest participation at Mass, however, means that we also take home with us something of what we have celebrated together. During the week we can continue to reflect on God's Word. This is very important to do. The Bible is not just to be analyzed and studied. It must become more real than other words we hear. This is a great challenge, since in our culture we are bombarded with the spoken word.

We have to decide which words will guide our lives. These will be the words we spend time with. As we go through the week and find ourselves in different situations at work, home, school, or recreation, we are called to remember what God has said and done. It is essential to breathe life into the words we have listened to by allowing them to influence our life.

While the Bible is the most published book in the world, it needs to be used in order to have any benefit. Every hotel has one. Every traveler needs one. May God's Word help us continue our journey.